Dancing in the Wonder

for 102 Years

An Autobigraphy

Marilee Shapiro Asher
with Linda Hansell

Ordering Information:
Available in paperback from Amazon.com and CreateSpace.com
Available on Kindle and other devices.

TABLE OF CONTENTS

Front cover:
Marilee Shapiro Asher
Playmates 1985
Bronze
6" x 6.5" x 3"

DEDICATION

For my family and good friends.

I passed the century mark, two years ago.
I feel so happy today, at age 102.
The sky, the air… (Ritalin helps.)

"The snail's on the thorn
God's in His Heaven —
All's right with the world!"

[From *Pippa Passes*, a poem by Robert Browning.]

— ◇ —

Presuming therefore that God is in His Heaven,
I write this:

DEAR GOD,

I DON'T KNOW WHO YOU ARE OR WHERE YOU ARE
OR IF YOU ARE.

BUT I DO WANT TO THANK YOU FOR MY LIFE,
AND ALL THE PERKS I HAVE ENJOYED.

I WANT TO THANK YOU ALSO FOR THIRTY MORE
YEARS THAN ARE USUALLY ALLOTTED, ACCORDING
TO YOUR BIBLE. I HOPE I HAVEN'T OVERSTAYED
MY WELCOME.

SINCERELY,

MARILEE

INTRODUCTION

I offered to help Marilee put this book together because of my deep affection for her, and because she has a fascinating story to tell. Marilee has been a wonderful presence in my life since I met her 18 years ago. Marilee is my first-cousin twice removed, as she is my grandfather's first cousin, on my mother's side. Due to a family rift that occurred in the Harris family in 1924 (that Marilee discusses in the book), my family never knew she existed until 1997. That year, her nephew John Harris contacted my mother and said "Did you know that you have a cousin that lives a mile away from you in Washington DC?" Marilee and my mother met soon afterward, and immediately formed a strong connection. Since that time, she has become an integral and much-loved part of our family.

Currently 102 years old, Marilee still has a wry sense of humor and a spring in her step. Although her longevity is one of the most salient features of her life, it is her lively personality (she is vivacious, resilient, perceptive, and sharp), her wit, her artistic accomplishments, her interest in esoteric ideas such as Greek mythology, Zen, and the Gurdjieff work, and the incredible span of history she has witnessed that make her a unique and fascinating individual. She attends exercise and yoga classes every week, and continues to learn and master new technologies—perhaps elements of the secret to her longevity.

A few years ago, Marilee started writing memories of her childhood and youth growing up in Chicago in the early part of the 20th century, which were published in a booklet by her nephew John Harris.[1] She got such a positive reaction to this endeavor from her family and friends that she wrote down more memories, this time of her adult life.[2]

These reminiscences were written as short vignettes. I felt there was more of the story to tell. Marilee and I worked together to fill in missing details and expand on the small tidbits she had enticed us with in the two booklets. Through interviews with Marilee and my own research, I have tried to bring to life the social and cultural contexts that frame her recollections.

From her birth in 1912 and her upbringing in a financially privileged family, through her years establishing herself as an artist and sculptor in the Chicago and Washington art scenes (despite the sexism that was prevalent in the art world in the 1940's, 50's and 60's,) through anecdotes of her family life and her reflections on her fifty years of participation in the Gurdjieff work, this book tells Marilee's story in fuller detail.

Linda and Marilee, December 2013.

It has been my great honor and privilege to work on this book with Marilee. We learned and laughed together as we journeyed through these vignettes and the accompanying photographs that evoke the colorful social and personal events that she has experienced in her creative and dynamic life.

LINDA HANSELL, *January 27, 2015*

ACKNOWLEDGMENTS

To my friends in Philadelphia and scattered around the county, and the members of my UUCR congregation in Philadelphia, thank you for journeying with me on this project.

Deep thanks go to Mary Marks, Mel Marks and Pam Marks Gartner for taking me on a tour of Marilee's birthplace in the Kenwood and Hyde Park neighborhoods in Chicago, and for helpful suggestions on the book.

My sincere thanks to Bradley Hess for his skillful editing of the manuscript, and his forbearance with instances of unconventional but intentional word usage and grammar.

To my wonderful family—my father, Herbert Hansell, my brother David Hansell, his partner Rob Cimino, my sister-in-law, Andrea Hansell, and my niece and nephew, Julie Hansell and Adam Hansell, thank you for your unwavering support and encouragement during this project, and always. I am extremely grateful to Rob for generously sharing his extensive collection of original Chicago House Wrecking Company and Harris Brothers catalogs. To my dearly-missed mother, Jeanne Harris Hansell, and brother, Jim Harris Hansell, your love is always with me, as mine is with you.

I am most indebted to John Harris (formally referenced in the book as Leo J. Harris) for his invaluable help with this book. In addition to publishing the two booklets of Marilee's reminiscences that were the impetus for this book, he graciously gave me access to, and personally curated for me, his extensive archives of Harris family history. I am also grateful to him for his permission to use material from his well-researched and highly informative articles on the Chicago House Wrecking Company and the Harris Brothers Company. For his help, support and hospitality, along with that of his wife Molly, I am most appreciative.

—L.H.

Dancing in the dark 'til the tune ends,
We're dancing in the dark and it soon ends,
We're waltzing in the wonder of why we're here,
Time hurries by, we're here and gone;

Looking for the light of a new love,
To brighten up the night, I have you love,
And we can face the music together,
Dancing in the dark.

1

FIRST MEMORIES

Do you know where babies come from? I was taught by my parents—and I believed—that "they" put a lot of sugar on the windowsill, and, in return for the sugar, the stork brought me. But I guess my mother didn't believe that, because in early 1912 she discovered to her dismay that I was on the way. This distressed her greatly, because she was 42 years old, and a proper Victorian woman did not have children in her forties.

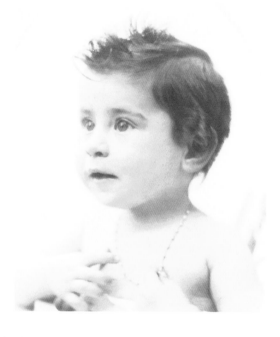

Why? Because it meant that she had done "the unmentionable" in her forties.

She tried to abort me by drinking castor oil. When this failed, my Aunt Lettie and Uncle Ben came to the rescue with a bona-fide offer: "Don't worry, Bonnie, we will take the child." Mother didn't take them up on it.

And so at 6:37 A.M. on Sunday, November 17, 1912, in Aunt Annie's room on the second floor of our house at 5000 Ellis Avenue in Chicago, I became a new member of the twentieth century. I think I was born in Aunt Annie's room because my mother didn't want to mess up her and Father's bed.

Me with Miss Stewart.

Snack on the beach
Wildwood, NJ 1914.

Up From the Gutter

At age two weeks, I ventured outdoors. Wrapped warmly in my buggy, as Mother watched from her upstairs window, my nurse, Miss Stewart, gently lowered the buggy down several stone steps. How it came about I do not know, but the buggy got away from her and overturned in the gutter.

It has been a long way up.

Miss Stewart

I was two and a half when my beloved nurse, Miss Stewart, left. I loved her so much that after she left I added a special blessing in my nighttime prayers.

After she left, when it was bedtime, my Aunt Annie bathed me, and if the occasion demanded, rolled up my long straight black hair on bean-shaped, white kidskin curlers. (They must have had wire inside.) Once I was in bed, Mother was called up from downstairs. She bent over me as she said our nightly prayer:

"May the Lord bless you and keep you, and raise His countenance upon you and grant you peace."

I replied:

> *"Now I lay me down to sleep*
> *I pray the Lord my soul to keep*
> *If I should die before I wake*
> *I pray the Lord my soul to take."*
> (So far so good.)

Then I continued: "God bless Mother, Father, Harvey, Francis, Imogene, Eleanor, and the Morris' chauffeur." After Miss Stewart left me, she worked for the Morris family, and their chauffeur would bring her to visit me. Hence, my prayer for him.

Pom Pom

When I was about three years old, my Uncle Jake (my mother's brother) brought me a truly life-enhancing gift. It was a small, fluffy, white female poodle. One of her hind legs was per-

True love. Pom Pom and me.

manently curled under her, and the fur of that leg was brown. She didn't seem to mind, and did well on three legs. I named her Pom Pom. Pom Pom spent a lot of time in my doll carriage wearing a bonnet and dress. She was very patient.

One day when I was about 10 years old, I was standing in the kitchen. I saw my Aunt Annie coming down the back stairs carrying Pom Pom wrapped in a newspaper. She had slipped her mortal coil.

* * *

Mother had two superstitions: 1) never walk under a ladder, and 2) you must not have thirteen people at the table. (Little did she know that the second superstition came from the Last Supper—Judas and all that.) From early on, I would either be fed in the kitchen or added, in my highchair, to make fourteen at the table in the dining room. What mighty power I held to avert disaster!

One Saturday when I was about four, dressed up for a special occasion, Father took me to lunch, just the two of us. We went to the Blackstone Hotel, Chicago's number one hotel. I somehow knew that the waiters knew about me and that he was showing me off. I had tomato soup and a lamb chop. I felt special that day. It is one of my fondest memories of my father.

Me "driving" the Pierce Arrow.

The family car was a Pierce Arrow. The Pierce Arrow was a huge touring car, the same type President Woodrow Wilson had. It seated seven, with two jump seats. I could walk from the back seat to the front two seats, which were separated by an aisle between. Canvas drop-down shades with isinglass inserts could close the open sides when it rained. (Isinglass is what we now call plastic.) A wide running board on each side made it easy to get in.

Eleanor complained that sometimes, since I liked to take my nap in the car, it wasn't available for other trips. Indeed, to facilitate my naps, the chauffeur had to drive the car around and around in Washington Park. The above sounds exaggerated to say the least. Some said I was "spoiled rotten."

Rite of Passage

As a child in the early 1900's, when one had had a sufficient number of colds and sore throats, one was entitled to a tonsil-lectomy and adenoid removal. This was "de rigueur" in those days. Luckily, I kept my adenoids and, I might add, they have never given me an ounce of trouble in 102 years.

However, I did have my tonsils removed. I remember I was on a gurney in front of the operating room at Michael Reese Hospital. My brother Francis came to see me. Then they tried

Very serious business—with my brother Harvey at the beach.

to smother me with a stinking cloth (the method of anesthesia), but I fought back.

When I woke up in bed, Mother was standing on one side of my bed, Miss Stewart on the other. I remember saying, "I thought I was going to die." How they exchanged looks!

When I got home I slept in the huge curly-cued brass bed with Father. Mother slept on the couch nearby. I wore my beautiful pale green silk nightgown with the wide lace collar. Father smelled of cigars.

Opera Night

Monday night was Opera night. I can see Mother, Father, and my sister Imogene (sixteen years older than I was) in their evening dress attire ready to go to the opera.

"I wanna go, too," I cried.

"No," says Aunt Annie, "you are going to a feather ball."

A feather ball meant a ball for royalty at which ladies wore a feather in their headdress—or, for me, to bed with a feather pillow. What a cruel jest!

Haute Couture:
me in 1917 Army outfit.

Reprimand, circa 1918

I was accustomed to being taken to school by Father on the way to his office. One day, a letter came from my brother Harvey, who was serving as a lieutenant in the Tank Corps at the front in France during World War I. Getting a letter from Harvey was a momentous occasion. Everybody gathered in the front hall to listen as the letter was being read aloud to the family.

I was going to be late for school, and I was carrying on and crying and stamping. Father raised an angry voice and shut me up. It stands out as the only time he ever uttered harsh words to me or yelled at me, and that stayed with me.

Scarlet Fever

When I was 11 years old, I had scarlet fever. The doctor came to the house. In those days you were treated at home. I wrote a letter, from my bed, to my dear friend Louise Greensfelder who was in Charlevoix, Michigan for the summer. Her father, who was a very well known doctor in Chicago, was horrified at the fact that I had sent a letter saying "I have scarlet fever." He, of course, destroyed it immediately, afraid that it could be communicated through the letter.

Change of Seasons

Sometime in mid-May, just when the white snowball bushes under the library windows burst into bloom, I too burst out: I burst out of my winter underwear. What freedom! The feeling of lightness fairly lifted me off the ground as I ran.

All summer, the lace curtains in the house would sway in occasional breezes by open windows. But then one day I would come home to another world. It came unannounced, vaguely familiar, full of portent of unknown change. The winter drapes were up.

In late summer and early fall came "putting up" time. Mother, Aunt Annie and Aunt Ray went in our car to the outskirts of town to buy directly from the farmers. These excursions to the farm were what probably led me to ask the quintessential logical question: "Do pigs lay bacon?"

They bought grapes and berries—including my favorites, currant and blackberry—to "put up" in glass jars. An empty flour sack, bloated with cooked and mashed fruit, dripped juice into a bucket next to the sink. A huge barrel in the pantry was full of pickles getting dilled. A rock on top of a plate on the barrel held the pickles down in the brine.

On cold winter mornings, I awoke and listened to the tinkling crackle of ice as the wooden wheels of the milk wagon went by. The milk wagon would deliver quart-glass bottles of milk, and the top two-and-a-half to three inches was a different color because it was cream. Later on, the milk bottlers got more sophisticated, and they sent a little plastic, carved spoon with the bottle so that you could reach in and scoop out the cream.

From time to time I have tried my hand at writing the Japanese form of poetry called haiku. I wrote a haiku poem about the early morning delivery of milk by wagon and horse:

> Cracking ice tinkles
> Under grinding wagon wheels
> Milk on our doorstep

In winter, the fire department would come and flood the backyard, turning it into a bumpy skating rink. I certainly was no skater. I was OK on two-runner skates, but when I graduated to regular shoe skates with one blade, my inner anklebone acted as though it was the second runner. I gave up ice-skating.

How it Was

Mail was delivered twice a day. We had a telephone in the hallway. When you picked up the phone, the operator said, "Number, please," and then you gave the number. If you had any problem, whenever you picked up the phone, the operator was there to help you. So you had direct contact. When I was maybe six or seven or eight, I used the telephone to talk to my friends, and I remember I used to take the phone into a nearby closet and close the door for privacy. I would have long conversations with kids in the neighborhood.

All year round, "the ice man cometh" in a horse-drawn wagon. The ice, 50 or 100 pounds of it, was carried on the iceman's back over a leather pad that he wore. He handled the ice with very large tongs when he came into the kitchen and placed the ice in the upper part of the icebox. In the neighborhood it was exciting and great fun to chase the wagon and steal ice chips.

Once a week, an Italian man with a horse-drawn wagon selling vegetables would come down the street. He always had lots of kids and kittens with him, and I remember that they gave me a kitten once. His children would be hanging on the wagon. That was an event I always enjoyed watching.

My Aunt Annie was the *majordomo* of the household, and she would go out and buy vegetables from the vegetable man. She also was the one that dealt with the butcher. She would take me in the car to the butcher shop very often while she purchased. Then she and Mother would make out the menus for the week. There were eight family members living in the house—my parents, the five of us children, and Aunt Annie—and two or three live-in help, so menu planning was considerable.

There were also men that came through the alley with a horse and buggy calling out in a song, what sounded like "Rags-a-lion, Rags-a-lion." "Rags-a-lion," I finally learned when I was maybe 15 years old, meant "rags and old iron," which is what they were selling. But I always heard it as "Rags-a-lion."

There were also beggars that came to the door. The cook would give them a plate of food, which they ate sitting on the back porch.

Halloween was the event of the year. We soaped windows, and we bobbed for apples. My friend and I used to spend hours making our own confetti, cutting paper in little pieces to throw and scatter in the neighborhood, on people's porches, or wherever. There was a lot of mischief. There was no trick-or-treating, like they do now to get candy. On Halloween night, people would just go out and do pranks. We put pins in everybody's doorbells. We'd stick a pin in the doorbell, and the bell would just keep ringing, ringing, ringing, ringing…. However, there was one house on our block where the elderly Woodhead sisters lived, and nobody ever touched their house. This was honor among thieves, so to speak.

More Mischief-Making

I was not a little angel. My friends and I enjoyed playing pranks on people. One day my friends and I took a pair of silk stockings and made runs in it everywhere, to the point it almost looked like a net. Then we wrapped it up as well as we could with fancy paper and bows to make it look like a gift, and delivered it to a house we didn't know. When the maid came to the door, we said, "This is for the lady of the house."

Another prank we played was that we used to answer employment advertisements for maids in the newspaper. We would call the number in the ad, give a false name and mimic a foreign accent, and make phony appointments for interviews.

Jewish Valkyrie

When the electric Victrola in our main hall played the recording of Wagner's "Ride of the Valkyries," my sister Eleanor would place the dog's leash between my teeth while she held the reins. AND OFF WE FLEW!

Round and round, galloping through the breakfast room, dining room, back through the hall into the library, into the parlor and back to the hall for more rounds. To this day that music still excites me.

Other Members of the Household

Jehu (of blessed memory) was our cherished handyman. He was from Jamaica. Gentle and kind, he wore part of a silk stocking on his head. In springtime, he took the oriental rugs out into the back yard and beat them with heavy wire attached to a wooden handle. The rest of the year he vacuumed the carpets. When Jehu died, Mother paid for his funeral.

Ellen, our housekeeper, was Norwegian. She started working for us when I was about eight. She served us at the table, made beds, and dusted. On her day off, looking very stylish with her fox fur around her neck, she patronized the finest clothing stores. We never knew much about her. Why was she a housemaid while we saw pictures of her family on their pleasure boat in Norway?

In 1935 Ellen began to show signs of dementia. She accused Mother of stealing her handkerchiefs and tried to commit suicide by drinking a bottle of Odorono, a deodorant. Luckily, a Norwegian friend took her home. Her family never answered Mother's inquiries as to how she was doing once she returned home.

I remember the end of World War I quite vividly. Both my brothers were overseas. My Aunt Annie, my mother's sister, lived with us all her life. I remember her going out on Ellis Avenue with a tremendous dishpan and a big spoon on the day the war ended and banging the pan, making lots of noise. People were going crazy celebrating the armistice. The first one was a false one, as it wasn't really true until about four days later. I remember being carried downtown on my father's shoulders to the Congress Hotel for the celebration of the armistice.

The Backyard

A large part of my childhood was played out in our backyard. There were many facets to it. There was a swing, a teeter-totter, a slide, and a sandbox. There was no end of possibilities with the teeter-totter. You could go up and down with someone on the other end, you "could walk the plank," or be otherwise creative.

Playing in the backyard.

There was a gang of neighborhood boys from the other side of the block. Mel Pfaelzer, later Rita Weil's husband, was a member. They would invade our backyard. Mel used to love to tell how Aunt Annie would come out with a broom and chase them away.

Then there was "under the porch," a dark, dank, three-sided cave for mixing various concoctions, early smoking experiments and hiding. One day my friend Joanne came over to play and, responding to nature's call, let go there. I went inside to fetch toilet paper. Meanwhile, inside, Mother's group of cousins was meeting with their embroidery in hand. "Joanne needs toilet paper," I loudly proclaimed. There was some consternation, as I recall.

When I was age ten or eleven I spent endless hours batting a tennis ball against the back brick wall.

It was a very easy, open way to live. I was not watched. I had the run of the neighborhood. I knew the alley system of our block. I rode my bike freely when I was eight years old or so.

My Early Sculptures, circa 1924

It was the dead of winter in Chicago. Everything was frozen solid. I had been collecting jelly glasses in many sizes and shapes. I filled them with water, colored with inks, and froze them on my windowsill. Once they were frozen, I ran the frozen jars under warm water just enough to release the beautiful, colored ice sculptures, and created a glamorous "installation" on my windowsill.

My reward for my early artistic endeavors was the flu.

Piano Lessons

I studied piano from age eight to sixteen. My first teacher was Ora Rimes, a sweet, pretty lady who soon got married and passed me along to Opal Felkner, a serious teacher. When she felt I was ready, she sent me to her teacher, Mrs. Murdoch, at the Columbia School of Music.

I remember playing a few Chopin preludes and some MacDowell, and a very contemporary, impressionistic "May Night," by Selim Palmgren. At the end of each season there would be a concert by Miss Felkner's pupils at our house. Another pupil, Babette Stein, somehow cut her finger during her rendition, and so the rest of us had to play our pieces on bloody keys. Ugh!

Although I played fairly well, I stopped taking lessons when I was 16. I didn't want to practice for hours upon hours. I did still play some after I married. The piano from our house on Ellis Avenue, a Steinway grand in a Circassian walnut case, travelled with me to Washington. I remember that as a young married woman, at around 6:00 in the evening I would say to myself, "Bernie (my husband) is coming home now from the office," so I'd start practicing!

Eventually I sold the piano for $1,000.

Our Dressmaker

Miss Burke was a tall, well-corseted, prim seamstress. Every now and then she showed up for a few days or a week . She was "Burkie" behind her back. She spent the day on alterations, or on a whole new dress from a pattern. She presided over the "sewing room." This was a long, narrow room on the second floor. At the end of the room in front of a window stood a foot-pedaled Singer sewing machine, and to the left an ironing table. To the right, the long wall was filled with floor to ceiling cabinets called the "linen closet."

Her nemesis was my sister Eleanor, who on occasion designed her own dress without a pattern and wanted Miss Burke to make it. She made poor Miss Burke cry.

A particular design of Eleanor's was an off-white silk sleeveless evening dress with a very full skirt down to her ankles. Around the waist, a Chinese embroidered belt continued all the way down the front to the hem, which was banded with white fur. I thought it was gorgeous. I often sat on Eleanor's padlocked chest and watched her get dressed to go out.

Miss Burke would sit with us at the lunch table. She ate copiously. She burped a lot. With her mouth full of pins she fitted us, and close up, her breath was not always sweet.

Confirmation

When I was twelve, Father walked me to The Temple, our synagogue, Isaiah Israel Congregation, that was two blocks away. A Chicago Landmark building, it still stands (now called KAM Isaiah Israel after a merger with Kehilath Anshe Maarav) on the corner of Hyde Park Boulevard and Greenwood Avenue, right across the street from President Barack Obama's home.

Father told Dr. Joseph Stoltz (not called Rabbi in reform congregations in those days) that he better take me in the confirmation class at age 12 or he might not get me later. The traditional age for confirmation is thirteen, and I would not be thirteen until November.

My selection to read was from the Book of Isaiah, Chapter 6, Verse 8. It was, "Here am I; send me." Where, and for what, I never found out.

Questions like these have led me on "a merry chase." Later you will see where my search has led me.

2

MY SCHOOLING

From Victorian School Mistresses to Dewey's Progressive Education

I started first grade when I was still five years old, as my birthday was in November. I attended the Faulkner School for Girls from first grade through tenth grade. The Faulkner School was eight blocks away from our house. Until I was in sixth grade, our chauffeur drove Father and me to school in the Pierce Arrow touring car. After that I walked to school.

In first grade, each day when we got there, my father took me inside and, while I sat on the stairs, he gently took off my coat and hung it up. Miss Austin, my first grade teacher, said that he was the most caring father she had ever seen.

My first day of school.

At the beginning of the year in first grade, I was scared and I would not stay at school alone at first. My older sister Imogene had to sit in the back of the room for two weeks until I would go it alone. Perhaps this is partially due to the fact that I was still five years old.

Miss Austin taught 1st and 2nd grades. She was a kind, prim lady. We practiced the "Palmer Method" of penmanship. This meant drawing on the blackboard ovals like this:

Some people could make them all fit together perfectly. I never could.

Although it was the Faulker School for Girls, there were boys in 1st and 2nd grades. The boy at the desk behind me used to pull my long braids.

The school was a dark brick building and it had a gymnasium in which we would play basketball and do Dalcroze. There was a little play yard in back with swings and a teeter-totter. There was a general assembly room with an upright piano. The teachers were female, single, gray-haired ladies.

Miss Faulkner, the head of the school, was very intimidating and very scary to me. She had one eye that was very unusual. The pupil was blue and white, with the colors all mixed up. It wasn't like a pupil. It was like a cloud formation, partly white and partly blue. When she looked at you, you couldn't help but look at it. She wore ankle-length, black, loose dresses with a touch of lace at the neck. Standing on a raised dais, her one sightless eye all mixed up blue and white, she would lead us in the Lord's Prayer:

"OUR FATHER (or Elizabeth Faulkner)…LEAD US NOT INTO TEMPTATION."

Day of Terror (4th grade)

Ah! The first day of snow! Louise Greensfelder (my second best friend) and I, intoxicated by the flakes, walked home from school, forgetting that our car was waiting for me at school. Arriving at home, I was told, "you MUST telephone school and ask them to inform the chauffeur to come home." The humiliation, the fear made the call something I could not, dared not, do. It was too awful. So my intrepid friend, Louise, impersonating me, made the dreaded call.

Some years later I realized it was really I who was, and would forever be, the CULPRIT in the eyes of Elizabeth Faulkner, the all powerful, stern headmistress, principal and owner of the school.

The Latin teacher at the Faulkner School, Ms. Canfield, was wonderful. I loved her. She was always dressed in a sloppy, gray, loose-fitting dress with chain necklace around her neck. Ms. Multon, the English teacher was rather terrifying to me. I felt she didn't like me, and I wondered if this was because I was Jewish.

One day in her class we were reading Ivanhoe, and one of the characters went to a nunnery. Being a little smart aleck, and knowing what I was doing, I raised my hand and I said, "Is there also a monkery?" She slapped me down pretty quickly.

The school rules were very strict. We wore uniforms, which were navy blue dresses—wool in winter, and silk in spring. One weekend a year there was a Field Day, which was a special event in which we did gymnastics, and the parents were invited. If you didn't attend it, you were expelled, which is what happened to two good friends of mine. In my sophomore year, my classmates Rita Weil and Dorothy Dottenheim, who were very beautiful girls, were invited to an out-of-town college fraternity party by some boys

This is the building that once housed the Faulkner School for Girls in Chicago. It now houses The Ancona School. Photo taken October 6, 2014.

they knew. It happened to be on the same weekend as Field Day at the Faulkner School. They went to the fraternity party, and they were expelled from the school. Rabbi Mann of the Sinai Temple in Chicago got involved, because this was looked upon as anti-Semitic. I don't recall the outcome.

It was a school in which the recognition of privilege was referred to as *noblesse oblige*. We were reminded frequently that we were privileged, and therefore had obligations.

High School

My father had believed in co-education, so in my junior year I changed schools. This was a posthumous move made to honor his wishes. I left the Faulkner School for Girls where I had started in first grade and entered University High School as a junior. It was the laboratory school of the University of Chicago, now known as the Lab School. Then, it was called University High School.

I had received a wonderful, basic, classical education at Faulkner. They excelled at teaching Latin and grammar. I left Faulkner well versed in Latin syntax, English figures of speech, and the diagramming of sentences. We learned about the lives and loves of every Greek God and Goddess, and we read Homer's Odyssey.

But it did not prepare me for University High School (U. High) to which I transferred, which was based on the progressive educational ideas of John Dewey, Francis Parker, and University of Chicago President William Rainey Harper. At Faulkner, we read Virgil to be able to diagram the sentence and to conjugate verbs in Latin. At U. High, they read Virgil, not for the grammar, but to get the meaning of it. U. High was much more about creative expression. The change from Faulkner to University High felt like going from the Victorian era into 2060, with no preparation.

Being the new girl in the 11th grade wasn't easy. There was not a lot of mixing between Jewish girls and non-Jewish girls. There were fourteen Jewish girls in my class, who had mostly gone through the previous grades together. It was a close-knit group, and although I ate with them and was invited to their parties, I felt I was never really accepted into their inner circle. We brought our lunches and ate together in the "girls club." One girl lived at a very upscale hotel and brought caviar sandwiches. I pretty much stuck to peanut butter and jelly or egg salad.

One day Miss Smithies, the girls' principal, called me into her office and inquired why the Jewish girls always ate together. I certainly had no answer, except that this was the way it was, since the Gentile girls all ate together. Case closed.

It was a mixed bag of plusses and minuses at U. High. As I mentioned, at U. High the philosophy of learning was based upon the ideas of John Dewey. No more reading "Ivanhoe" by Sir Walter Scott in English class, but instead we read living authors and poets.

A big difference between the two schools was the music program at each school. At Faulkner School for Girls, the music program had consisted of gathering in the gymnasium and singing songs like "The Bells of Saint Mary's, I Hear They are Calling," and "Pale Hands I Loved Beside the Shalimar." They also had us learn—and this I value—Wagner's *Der Ring des Nibelungen (The Ring of the Nibelung)* which is in German. We learned the whole thing—the story, the characters, and to associate the characters with the music.

When I got to U. High, music class was very different. Music appreciation with Mr. Vail was a joy. We wrote our own songs. I wrote mine to the A. A. Milne poem, "Three Friends." Here it is:

> *Ernest was an elephant a great big fellow*
> *Leonard was a lion with a six-foot tail   (glissando)*
> *George was a goat and his beard was yellow*
> *And James was a very small snail.*

U. High was an encounter of a far different kind. My world had become less knowable, less secure, but more interesting.

Grand Tour

In July 1919, we sailed on the Cunard-line ship "Aquitania" for Cherbourg. We were five: Mother, Father, Imogene, Eleanor and me. Along with us were Mr. and Mrs. Bowers, (Father's banker friend from New York) and their daughter Phyllis, age 13; and Nate and Belle Harris with two sons, Joseph, age 18 and Jerry, age 9. (Nate was Uncle Ben Harris' brother. Ben Harris was Aunt Lettie's husband but not related to us).

Aunt Annie, who was sick with heart trouble, was left at home in the care of Miss Stewart. Aunt Annie had made the clothes for a doll she gave me when we left, and I remember she cried fearing she would never see me again. She lived until I was sixteen.

Father and me in Paris, 1919.

First stop was London, where we visited cousins of Mother's whose family name was Rosenbaum. We had tea at their house with a very old lady.

We stayed at the Savoy Hotel in London, where my diary reports that they had the best down quilts I had ever experienced.

Then followed Belgium, Germany, and France in a rented car with a driver named Rex. We toured the battlefields of World War I, where my brother Harvey's Tank Corps had seen action.

Then we went on to Paris for a month. At the Majestic Hotel in Paris we had a suite: living room, dining room and three bedrooms. I had my own tiny room, but I was too scared at night most of the time to sleep in it, and would crawl in bed with my parents. Mother let me sleep next to her.

Madame DuBroise, an elegant French war widow, was hired to be my governess. I was provided with a hoop and a stick to roll in the Bois de Boulogne. This was not my idea of fun. So Madame became guide and companion for Mother. She knew Paris, she knew where to buy everything, and Mother did buy: clothes from the famous houses for my sisters, a peach colored coat for me, gloves, tapestries, lace, furniture, tortoise shell and ivory painted boxes, and more.

Madame DuBroise's stylish hats were made of woven paper. That was all they had to work with after the First World War. She had an ancestor who was an officer in the American Revolution, and therefore she was entitled to be a member of the Society of the Cincinnati. Eleanor and I tried to help her achieve her goal, but without success.

During World War II, Eleanor sent her packages and later, when Eleanor and her husband Leo went to Paris, they saw her again.

Mrs. Weil, the mother of my friend, Rita, later met Madame DuBroise, who was then working in the gift shop at the Louvre. Small world syndrome!

Father and me in the fields in France.

Eleanor and I saw her for the last time in 1962, visiting her in the tiny rooms in Paris where she lived alone.

Madame's obituary was published in the newspapers because of her attempts to sue for the royalties on Baudelaire's work. Her claim was based on the fact that she had inherited the copyright from her uncle, who had been Baudelaire's publisher. Unfortunately, she was no more successful in this endeavor than she was in being accepted by the Society of the Cincinnati.

A forgotten skill, in Paris.

Right now, I can feel myself in that Paris hotel room after breakfast, as she jauntily, gaily, happily enters with "Bonjour, mes enfants," followed by our flat, American "Bonjour Madame." She was the quintessential Parisienne who knew everything and where it was.

Coming of Age

When I was fifteen, somewhere I met one of those smart, bespectacled, nerdy boys who gave me a paperback by Margaret Mead, called *Coming of Age in Samoa*. I guess I had refused his advances, and he was justifying himself by showing me how it was done in Samoa. (Yeah, but not with you, Buddy.)

At about the same age, at a party at a girl friend's home there was an "older man" of nineteen or twenty. The turn of conversation caused me to say (I am actually blushing now), "I would rather have major surgery than intercourse." I meant it, too!

I was pretty sophisticated, I thought, at sixteen. One evening, my brother Harvey took me along to a gathering of a few of his friends at the home of his good friend, Walter Rubovitz. I remember I was wearing a navy blue suit with a pale blue satin blouse and a loose navy blue jacket, and that I wore my very long hair in braids around my head.

The assembled group was drinking. One man, quite in his cups and flirting with me, tried to pour wine in my shoe while preparing to make a toast. My embarrassed brother took me quickly home.

Beauty

My childhood best friend Charlotte Klein and I played beauty parlor. One day she gave me the ultimate facial. She put hot towels over my entire face, over which she placed a pillow to keep the heat in. This was followed by cold cloths. The process was repeated a number of times. Fortunately, Miss Stewart was staying with us then, taking care of Aunt Annie, so I got treatment for my first degree burn.

On another vividly recalled occasion, Charlotte and I stood side by side in front of her dresser mirror. She said, "I am prettier than you are!" I accepted that without argument. "But you have a nice smile," she added, tossing me a crumb.

Another time, when I was about fifteen, my gorgeous, very popular, very close friend Rita (Weil) Pfaelzer said to me "You look like Rebecca at the well." In a way it was a compliment. She didn't mean it in a nasty way. She'd seen illustrations of "Rebecca at the Well." She was commenting on the fact that my looks were Semitic. But I interpreted this to mean that I looked too Jewish.

I do not remember ever getting a compliment from my mother on how I looked. The nearest she came was that she "liked the way I carried my head, and I did always tell the truth." She admonished me, "You are not pretty, so you better be neat and clean." Is it any wonder why I never thought I was attractive?

Noses

All of us in the Harris family had very prominent noses. When I was very young, Eleanor and my cousin Frances Rothschild used to rub my nose, hoping to prevent me from developing the Harris bumped nose that ran in the family.

Everybody had an explanation for this hump bump on the nose. For example, one might say "I was hit by a field hockey ball, that is why my nose is like it is." Each one of us had a reason, which of course was not the real reason.

I remember one evening when I was about eight, my childhood chum Charlotte was at my house for dinner. Father was at the head of the table and everybody was there. She turned to him and said, "You remind me of Abraham Lincoln," and he sort of puffed himself up. She said, "You both have big noses."

Within the family, the nose was always a subject of humor among ourselves. It was talked about and joked about. But when I sat next to a very handsome boy in high school English class, I was unable to talk to him. I was very shy, and to have him next to me where he could see my profile was painful.

Vindication came at last. When I was twenty-three years old, Arturo Fallico, my first art teacher, said in Italian to his friend, speaking of me, "BELLA!"

WOW!

They say that if Cleopatra had had one more inch on her nose it might have changed the world. I can add two examples of life altering cases.

One Sunday, in 1936, my cousin Joanne Myers and I went downtown on the I.C. (Illinois Central railroad) train to an office building on Michigan Avenue. There, in an office, a "cosmetic surgeon" performed a nose job on my cousin. I was in the waiting room as he worked away, while in the operating room the radio blared the horse races. We taxied home to her unwelcoming parents.

The other case was my sister, Eleanor. Without telling anyone, she went to Cincinnati, where Dr. Samuel Iglauer was an early expert in nose jobs. She had no money, but the doctor took her pearls as collateral. (The doctor undoubtedly checked who her father was.) Eleanor came home all bandaged up.

In neither case did the new noses qualify as pretty, but they seemed to sniff, blow, and smell as good as ever, and made their new wearers happy.

3

MY CHILDHOOD HOME

Victorian and Romanesque in Granite

Our house was located at 5000 Ellis Avenue in the Kenwood neighborhood of Chicago, on the South side. It was built out of 18-inch-thick granite blocks that were salvaged from the old Chicago Post Office, which was dismantled by my grandfather, Moses

My childhood home: 5000 Ellis Avenue (far right).

Harris, along with my father and his brothers, through their company, the Chicago House Wrecking Company.

Construction on our house was started in 1899. The foundation for the house sat for a year before they started building, perhaps because the house was to be built of such heavy granite. It was completed in 1901 or 1902. The 18-inch thick granite blocks provided wonderful natural air conditioning. The house was always cool in summer.

Across the street there was a vacant lot, and there were cows there when they began to build. This gives a sense of how far out from downtown Chicago it was in those days. (It is approximately 6.3 miles due south of the Loop in the heart of downtown.)

The only effort at gardening was a row of pansies along some bushes separating us from the Harris house next door. I can now feel a summer morning walking along the pansy row with Father along side me, and handing him a pansy for his button hole before he went to the office.

The house was really quite grand, and very Victorian inside. There was a "great hall," as it was called in baronial castles. It was in the center of the main floor. The oriental carpet-covered staircase came down beside the Circassian walnut grand piano. Midway, the staircase paused for a landing, encircled by a bay window encasing three life size figurative stained glass windows. In front of them was a semi-circular cushioned seat.

There was a fireplace in which we threw crystals that made the fire turn colors. The floor was tiled in very small colorful mosaic patterns. In a corner stood an electric Victrola, housed in a large cabinet storing records of Caruso, other opera recordings, and popular jazz.

Another view of the house, with Mother's electric automobile by the front door.

In this background I performed my Narcissus dance. My sister Imogene was a first class pianist, and she played "To a Wild Rose" by MacDowell while I swayed around an imaginary pool, finally falling on my knees, falling in love with myself, and falling into the pool.

(Quite a lot of falling.)

I learned to fox trot with our often-present cousin, Frances Rothschild, (the daughter of Mother's sister, Rachel) who was ten years older than I. Father loved to dance. I would stand on his feet while he danced with me. He loved Puccini's Madame Butterfly, and I still get teary when I hear it.

The dining room was a perfect example of Victorian decor. A marble bust of a young girl called "Primavera" stood on the mantel over the fireplace. Nearby stood a life size bronze statue of "Hebe," cupbearer to the gods. Over a round mahogany dining room table hung a massive Tiffany chandelier. At one end of the room was a bay window area with cushioned seats. Here father would sit and listen to the squeaky Zenith radio.

The "great hall."

The dining room had a chandelier made of Tiffany glass.

The Parlor.

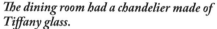

The parlor was a Victorian dream. A blue and rose-colored Oriental rug under a large crystal chandelier was background for Louis Quinze furniture. Gilded armchairs and a couch were covered with Aubusson tapestry. A fire screen had a tapestry scene of Othello and Desdemona.

Oddities on Ellis Avenue

Ellen Hoguestad, our housekeeper, was very fond of Polly, my parrot. She liked to take Polly for a walk down Ellis Avenue on a summer evening, with no tether between them. Polly followed her like a puppy dog, waddling along beside her. A touching (albeit unsanitary) exchange between Ellen and Polly was when Ellen, chewing a cracker, would offer a morsel to Polly from her own lips.

Catty corner across Ellis Avenue from us there lived a family named Freund. Mr. Freund was quite rich, having made his money in sausage casings. He had a small zoo in the back of their house, and their chimpanzee, dressed in a little sailor suit and riding a tricycle with his keeper beside him, was a great sight on the avenue.

We also contributed our share of eccentricities. When my brother Harvey returned from the First World War, he brought battlefield mementos in his trunk instead of clothes. Among the loot was a German machine gun. From the third floor turret window it was aimed straight down Ellis Avenue.

And there was more. The remainder of the battlefield mementos, which included live hand grenades, some bombs, field telephones, helmets, and other equipment, were kept in a third floor storage room. Every year, at spring-cleaning time, our faithful handyman, Jehu, carefully moved, dusted, and replaced the precious trove. (It could have blown up the house next door!)

However, when World War II came, it became the task for Eleanor and me to empty and ready the house for sale. Our first call was to Civil Defense to tell them about the ordnance in the attic. Alarmed, they said, "Get out and don't touch them!" They called the police, who called the fire department, and they put a cordon around the house.

Alas! The trove was removed and some was detonated.

We had radiators for heat, with containers that hung on the back with water in them to moisturize the air. The house was heated by coal, kept in a ceiling-high bin in the furnace room. A janitor or handyman shoveled coal twice a day into the furnace. I can hear Mother on the telephone ordering "Pocahontas Mine Run," a particular size and type of coal for heating. (The Pocohantas Coal Company still exists.)

I don't think I ever really knew the whole basement. There were two storerooms, and a bedroom and bath for a houseman. The laundry room had gas stoves to heat the irons for ironing. Later we had a mangle, an electric roller iron for sheets.

In a separate section with its own staircase leading up to the main hall was a large card room. Next to it was the billiard room. The green felt-covered pool table, the ivory balls in a wooden triangle, the little squares of chalk around the table edge, and the cues on the wall in a rack stood in readiness for the inveterate players—Father, my brothers Harvey and Francis, Uncle Ben (Aunt Lettie's husband), and Uncle Maurie (Aunt Ray's husband).

A door from the billiard room led into the dirt-floored wine cellar, which had been dug out under the front lawn.

The current building at 5000 Ellis Avenue. Photo taken October 6, 2014.

There was a "dumb waiter" from the basement to the third floor. Once we heard a terrible banging and knocking. Not bats in our belfry, but pigeons in the dumb waiter.

I hope I have conveyed what it was like to live in that remarkable house. I have actually wondered if something so real, so vivid, doesn't actually still exist somewhere in another reality. Eleanor felt the same way, since she would recall every detail as she walked through the house in her imagination.

It was a huge house. Although it cost $100,000 to build in 1900, my mother sold it at the height of the Depression for $10,000. It was lived in until the late 1950's or early 1960's, when it was abandoned and fell into disrepair. An article in the *Hyde Park Herald* on March 22, 1961 recounts: "The city filed suit in Superior Court last week to have the building at 5000 Ellis Avenue condemned. The old abandoned mansion is owned by Henry L. and Marie Balaban now residing in Florida.... According to James Hibbin of the Community Conservation Board...[t]enants have since moved out, and the owners have allowed the building to deteriorate to the point where it is both an eyesore and a hazard to the community."[1] It was torn down by the city of Chicago.

Now there is a newer, ranch-style house there. Quite a change!

Many of the homes that were on the block when I lived there are still there, and have been updated. And two blocks away is President and Michelle Obama's house.

The Times Get Tough

As the saying goes, teens are the pits. Mine certainly were. They started off with the death of my father in 1926. I was thirteen.

What had been my nuclear family soon changed dramatically. Soon after my father's death, my closest ally, my beloved older sister Eleanor married and left Chicago. My oldest sister Imogene was already married, and my brother Francis, too, had married and left the nest. My oldest brother, Harvey, had gone to work in a different city. What had been a family of seven—two parents, my four siblings, and me—gradually dwindled to Mother, Aunt Annie, our loyal housekeeper Ellen, and me.

The feel of our house changed after my father died. A gloom settled over the house. Before, the rooms were sunny. Now a moody, sullen light hung in each room. I see myself as thirteen years old, a freshman in high school, walking home from school down 50th Street. A block away I see the great grey granite turret of our house. I trudge towards it joylessly.

I am large—five and a half feet tall, sturdy, strong. I am a child inwardly mourning. I am unable to cry except in my bed at night. I tell myself I must be strong. I am his child. I wish I had been a boy like him, to be worthy of him. I cut my hair into a boyish bob. It was a painful time for me. Looking back, the word "aimless" comes to mind. This was probably depression.

I paint a gloomy picture, but there were also pleasures. I had many friends. I also enjoyed my visits to see my sister Eleanor, in Minneapolis, where she lived with her husband Leo and three young sons. Christmas visits and some summer vacations there were respites for me. There, besides being with my beloved sister, I developed a circle of close friends, who became my companions in becoming juvenile, intellectual snobs. That circle included Harry Levin who became the famous James Joyce scholar at Harvard University, Arthur Morton, who went to Hollywood to write musical scores for movies, and his brother Lawrence, a renowned musicologist and close friend of Igor Stravinsky. I earned my place in the group by naming "Toulouse Lautrec" for the category "artist whose name began with 'T'" in the endless

word games that we played.
We loved Ravel's "*Bolero*," and
we would put that record on the
Victrola and dance wildly
around the living room.

I learned to drive Eleanor's
Packard. On long summer
evenings I could drive to my
friend's house where a game of
ping-pong on the front porch
might be going on. These were
halcyon days for me.

In the late 1920's, many of
my friends were having their
pictures taken by the hot photographer at the time, James
Hargis Connelly, who achieved
fame for his photographs of
entertainers. I also had my photograph taken by him, and
somehow, this photograph
ended up in a display case for
picture frames at Marshall Fields department store!

Marshall Fields display photograph, 1929.

Prohibition

I came of age during Prohibition, and I remember going to speakeasies.
They did not feel like bad places. They let you in and you ordered whatever
you ordered, and that was it. It didn't feel underworld, except for one place
that I remember on Cottage Grove Avenue where they frisked you when you
came in. I think there was also gambling there.

My family had some stock in a liquor company called Grommes and
Ullrich. They produced Black Label Kentucky Straight Bourbon Whiskey.
When Prohibition came in, people that owned stock in the company were
given the value of their stock in kind. So one day, an armored Brink's truck
pulled up to our house and delivered barrels of whiskey. They were brought

in and put in our wine cellar. During the Prohibition years, this became my brothers' inexhaustible supply of the forbidden stuff, with which they filled their flasks. They replaced the amount taken with water, and the dilution went un-noticed for quite a time.

The Great Depression

In 1929 came the "Crash." That night the world changed. A friend's father jumped out of a window and killed himself, and not long after that her mother was found drowned in her bathtub, leaving my friend to take care of two younger siblings. There were other horror stories, too. My future husband Bernie had an uncle, a lovely man, who had to put paper in his shoes because he had holes in the soles, and could not afford new shoes.

As for us, we were no longer rich, as my mother had bought stocks on margin, and suffered a huge loss, but I can't say that we suffered. I did not have the clothes that I would like to have had, but I did not suffer. I was a freshman in college at the University of Chicago, and I continued to go to school. I lived at home, and walked to the University, about 1.5 miles away. I graduated from the University of Chicago in March of 1933. (My degree was a Ph.B., a Bachelor of Philosophy. They didn't use the term Bachelor of Arts at that time.)

During those years my mother would sew dresses for me. She sewed a lot, and I remember helping her to pull basting threads. One day I asked her "Do we save basting threads?" That was my understanding of the Depression—what to save.

My millionaire brother-in-law, Charles, Imogene's husband, lost his fortune and they, along with their two-year-old son Maurice, and his nurse, moved in with us.

After my father's death, the changed family configuration contributed to a change in my feelings about the house. It now felt heavy, dark, and old-fashioned. I would have preferred white walls, like my friends had in their houses. The house went from being the place where I lived contentedly and unquestioningly to becoming a place of gloom and confinement.

4

THE NUCLEUS OF MY FIRMAMENT

Mother, Father and Aunt Annie

Mother, Father and Aunt Annie formed the nucleus of my firmament, orbited by the five children.

My Mother, Bonnie Harris

Who in one's life could be more important than one's mother? Rebecca "Bonnie" Levine Harris was born in 1870 and

Father, Aunt Annie, Mother, me and Pom Pom on our back steps, circa 1916.

died in 1961. She was a Victorian lady who became free, towards the end of her life, through the power of her artistic creativity.

She was well read, well traveled, and an innate connoisseur of beautiful things. She loved and collected lace. Having the means, she filled our house with tapestries and Tiffany and Murano glass, the great crafts of our times.

But what about the relationship between us? She was always a selfless, dutiful mother to me, but not demonstrative or affectionate. I remember that she held my hand as we rode home in a taxi after meeting me at the train station on my return from two months at a summer camp in Maine. That this physical contact was memorable to me tells me of its emotional impact, and its uniqueness. The other similar, wonderful memory was of her embracing me when I came to see her in Chicago shortly before she died. She said she was so glad I was there. (This brings tears even now as I write.)

My mother (Bonnie Harris) at the turn of 20th century.

Her words of praise were scarce but golden to me: "Marilee always tells the truth," or, "I like the way she holds her head," or, "Marilee has kept me young."

I was kind of a nasty teenager in relation to her. I remember my resistance to her, my total lack of feeling and understanding for her. Only after I married did we become friends. I always respected her, but looking back, I ask myself if I loved her then. I think not.

I picture her, widowed at age 54, seated at her dressing room table, reading late into the night. She was born too bright and had the wrong gender for the limits of the Victorian times in which she lived. Not until she was 79 years old did she come into her own, when she discovered painting, having been urged to try it by my sister Eleanor.

In painting she found challenges, fulfillment and great joy. She was reborn, becoming eager, outgoing and warm. Traveling by air, carrying her large portfolio of paintings, she made the rounds, visiting with her five

Mother and me. Passport photo circa 1920.

children. She would spend winters in Washington with me, summers in Colorado at her son Harvey's ranch, and other times in Minneapolis or Chicago, divided between her two daughters Eleanor and Imogene, and son Francis.

She received considerable artistic acclaim, as evidenced by the fact that the following museums that have a Bonnie Harris painting in their permanent collection:

- Baltimore Museum of Art, Baltimore, Maryland.
- Smithsonian National Collection of American Art, Washington, D.C.
- The Phillips Collection, Washington, D.C.
- Folk Art Museum, New York City, New York.
- The Smart Museum, Chicago, Illinois.

A remarkable achievement for someone who did not start painting until the age of 79!

Mother's painting, "Houses in Winter (Minneapolis)." Bonnie Harris, 1953. Smithsonian American Art Museum Permanent Collection.

Father

My father, Frank Harris, was born in Chicago in 1868. His father, Moses Harris, was an immigrant from Policza, Poland who lived from 1840 to 1900. Moses must have come to America either during, or directly after, the Civil War. The fact that Ellis Island had not been opened yet makes it impossible to track on what boat or what date he arrived. My father was one of four sons—Abe, Sam, Frank, and Dave—and two daughters—Hattie and Sarah—of Moses Harris and Mary Leah Levy Harris.

My grandfather Moses was one of ten children. He died before I was born, but I knew his youngest brother, my great uncle Abe, very well, and I liked him very much. He was a darling man. Uncle Abe was a peddler, as Moses was initially. Uncle Abe came over to America at the age of twelve, and made his way to Minneapolis. The only thing that he ever told me about his life in Europe was that they had a dirt floor, but then everybody did in those days.

My father was mercurial, playful, and terribly bright. He had the kind of mind that could add columns of figures in his head, and he had many close men friends. He was also very family-oriented and warm, which was not a typical Harris family characteristic. I was just 13 when he died, so I only knew him as a child. He was certainly the parent that I loved and who was very playful with me.

My grandfather, Moses Harris, is second from the right in the back row.
He is pictured here with his nine siblings, a brother-in-law, and a pasted-in photo of my
great-grandfather, Lazar Vergransky, who became Louis Harris (far left, front row).

My father, Frank Harris, on a camping trip.

When he would take me to school my first year, he would come in with me and hang up my coat every day. I was bereft when he died. His death was the pivotal, deciding moment of my life.

He had only an 8th grade education, but could express himself well in writing, and was a successful businessman.

Father was not a mild mannered man, especially at the table if he did not like the food. He was fussy about food and he would complain. On one occasion, sitting next to him in my highchair while he loudly complained, I ordered him, "Eat the fish!" On another similar occasion, it is recorded, I said, "Let him scream it out. It's good for him." He laughed. Being a man used to giving orders, I think my father relished mine.

Once when he was pulling me on my sled in the snow, he lay down in the snow, flapping his arms to make me an angel. I was three or four, and still remember it vividly. By then he was about forty-eight years old.

In my mind's eye, I can see Father play Canfield (solitaire) after dinner in the evenings. Where was Mother?

I remember a Thanksgiving vignette, circa 1922. The round table is pulled out to its full oval capacity. We have guests. The turkey awaits us on the table. Polly, my parrot, rising to the occasion, is squawking in full voice amid the conversation of

Mother, Father, Harvey and Francis.

the assembled. Father is beginning to carve. Unnerved and exasperated, and wielding his mighty carving knife, with unprintable words he threatens Polly with decapitation. I am crying loudly. Polly and cage are removed from the room.

In 1920 or 1922, my father had an encounter with the spirit world. Ectoplasm, messages from the other side, and floating tables were all the rage. Father was persuaded to visit a great medium everyone was talking about. To be incognito, he took the streetcar to her place. She welcomed him and told him there was a message from his mother-in-law, thanking him for taking care of her daughters. (When Frances Myers Levine, my mother's mother died of a heart attack at age 44, Mother and Father took Mother's three much-younger sisters in to live with them: Lettie, Rachel, and Annie.) Father was startled that the medium would have known this.

The Fishing Trips

Every year, my father, my two brothers, and sometimes my Uncle Morry would go on a camping and fishing trip. They would go to the North Woods

Father with his catch.

The whole family on a fishing trip, 1913. I am 9 months old, being held by my nurse, Miss Stewart.

of Wisconsin for several weeks at a time. It was a big event each year, and there was much talk about it and much planning for it. They fished for muskies (also known as "ugly pike.") They always had a guide, who also cooked for them. We heard about "the great fish chowder" they ate.

When I was about nine months old, in 1913, the whole family went on the fishing trip, including Mother, my nurse Miss Stewart, and me.

I love this photo of my father play-acting as Robin Hood on

Father, playing Robin Hood.

one of his annual fishing trips. The fishing trips were the thing, I think, that he lived for. This picture of my father speaks to me about an earthiness that my father had that I did not see in his brothers.

I Lose Him

As I write this, I relive January of 1926. I was thirteen. Mother came into my bedroom in her nightgown. We sat on the window seat by the bay window. She told me Father was very sick. She was waiting for a specialist from Boston whom she had called to come. She told me the future was uncertain.

January 17th came and Miss Stewart called me to come and kiss my father goodbye. He lay turned away from me on his side, sweaty and breathing loudly. I leaned over and lightly kissed his wet forehead. He died that day. That night my mother sent me away to sleep at my cousins' house, the Myers. Although my cousins Joanne and Sissy (Virginia) were my frequent playmates, being sent to their house felt cruel and callous, because I wanted to be with my immediate family. I was bereft. I remember how Sissy looked at me silently with a frightened expression. She asked me if I wanted a glass of water.

The funeral took place at home. His coffin was placed in front of the marble fireplace in the parlor. Folding chairs were set up in rows for the family. Rabbi Stoltz, who had married my parents, officiated. I remember nothing that was said.

I sat in the second row and was painfully aware of my cousin Sam ("Junie") Harris, who was three years older than me. He lived next door and was my early childhood playmate. Two years before, my father had split from his brothers in a disagreement over the future of their business, Harris Brothers Company, and this schism was very confusing to me. Junie was on the other side of the split. At the time of the split two years prior, we had suddenly stopped playing, even speaking. Now, here he was.

After the service I ran upstairs to my room and sobbed. An uncle I hardly knew was sent up to my room where I was crying, to persuade me to go to the cemetery, which I was refusing to do. He was not a blood relative. He was the husband of an aunt and I felt no kinship with him. I did go to Rosehill Cemetery that day. Today, a very tall obelisk marks the plot where Father and Mother's descendents spend eternity.

As I look back at how my family treated me at that crisis in my life, I find it distressing. No one acknowledged my pain and deep grief. Nobody consoled or comforted me. They didn't think of what my feelings might be.

I was kept out of school in the house for a week. My sister Eleanor, the only one to recognize my grief, took me for a walk and said, "It will be over soon," referring to the house being full of people and condolences.

One day during that week Aunt Sarah, Father's older sister, was visiting. She was crying and telling how she had held him in her arms as a baby and saying something about God.

"I don't believe in God," I said. She was shocked.

My nightly prayer was addressed to Zeus, Jesus, and Jehovah. I prayed for them to give Papa a safe passage or journey. I did not specify whether to heaven, or across the river Lethe of Greek myth, with old, blind Charon and the dog Cerberus. I continued this for a whole year. This was my Kaddish.

Why, as a Jewish girl, did I include Jesus in my prayers? The Christmas stories, Christmas tree, and the Christmas Pageant at the Faulkner School for Girls were so beautiful and alluring that I wanted to be a part of it. I remember feeling that Jesus loved me, and my mother didn't know. But I believed in Zeus more than Jesus, I can assure you.

In my mourning, I got my hair cut into a boyish bob. I kept the combings from Father's hairbrush in an envelope in my drawer. I became a "poker face."

The cruelest cut of all was Mother saying "You are the coldest proposition I have ever seen. You have never shed a tear for your Father." If only someone had known how I was grieving inside, and how I cried alone in my bed. I am still making up for it.

One night around 1950, I had an apparition. I saw my father standing at the foot of my bed. He did not speak, just looked at me.

SO REAL. FATHER!

I have never again experienced such joy. It was a precious dream.

Aunt Annie

My Aunt Annie played a special role in my life, and was a great help to Mother in running a big household. She was my mother's sister who never married. She came to live with us after their parents died, and was a member of our household until she died.

Aunt Annie was the *majordomo* in the household. She would go out and buy vegetables from the vegetable man. She did the marketing and helped plan meals with my mother, and when she went to the butcher shop I often went along. She bought my shoes, bathed and dressed me, fed and generally supervised and bossed me. She was bright. She could fix mechanical things.

I did not have warm feelings towards Aunt Annie while I was growing up, but in later years, I have had very great remorse for not appreciating her. She died when I was about 16, and for all those years she was an important member of the household.

Aunt Annie, Eleanor and Harvey in a carriage.

5

SISTERS AND BROTHERS

My four older siblings were significantly older than me—a consequence of my being an unplanned baby and surprise pregnancy for my mother. Harvey, Francis, Imogene, and Eleanor were 20, 18, 16, and 14 years old, respectively, when I was born. They were almost another generation, but nevertheless played a huge role in my life, especially Eleanor and Harvey.

Eleanor

Where should I begin? My sister Eleanor is everywhere in me. From the first moments of my awareness, she was my favorite, as she was throughout my life until she died in 1993 at the age

My sister Eleanor as a young girl.

of 95. She was there at my beginning and, like the good fairy that attended the princess's birth bestowing gifts, Eleanor gave me her own gifts all her life. When I was little she played with me. When I was an adolescent, she comforted me. She became my mentor, teacher, role model, and best friend. She was my confidante, playmate, guide, alter ego, inspiration—she was everything to me. In short, she was the delight of my life. She was 14 years older than I.

I remember crawling into her bed with her on some early mornings. She would look up and point to the ceiling of the room. Around the concave curve that joined wall to ceiling were, in bas-relief, little girls holding garlands of flowers. She would call to them: "Dollies, come down, Marilee wants to play with you."

They looked like this:

They never did come down, but the idea was so exciting. Eleanor also said that fairies lived in her paint box. I remember looking, but they were never there when I looked.

Eleanor was a free spirited, intellectually gifted, and highly talented artist who was very avant-garde. She shocked the family with a padlocked box that she kept. It looked like a pirate's chest, but she upholstered the seat with some hand painted velvet she had made. It really bugged Aunt Annie that she kept it padlocked. No one ever knew the contents of the box.

As a cum laude graduate of Vassar College, she was awarded a fellowship in mathematics. But family pressures brought her home to Chicago. At Vassar, having broken out of the conventional mold, she smoked and bobbed her hair, which upset my mother greatly. She was far too liberal for our parents, with her leftish leanings

Eleanor.

and other unacceptable ideas. When I was ready to go to college, Mother said, "Vassar ruined one of my daughters. It won't ruin another." (I attended the University of Chicago, and lived at home.)

Another example of Eleanor's unconventionality was her frequent outings to the Dil Pickle Club in Chicago. The Dil Pickle Club (or Dill Pickle Club) was a popular bohemian club in Chicago that operated between 1917 and 1935, and functioned as a speakeasy, cabaret, and theatre where activists, political speakers and authors came to speak. The Dil Pickle Club was considered a forum for free thinkers. It hosted writers and speakers (including Clarence Darrow, Emma Goldman, Carl Sandburg, Sherwood Anderson, Vachel Lindsay, and Upton Sinclair) artists, intellectuals, prostitutes, and bums. Eleanor's participation was part of her nonconformist nature. The family, especially our somewhat sarcastic brother Francis, ridiculed and teased her for going there.

Glacier National Park

In the summer of 1922, my sisters Eleanor and Imogene and Imogene's husband, Charles took me to Glacier National Park. El and I shared a room at night, and she read Nietzsche's *Thus Spoke Zarathustra* to me. I listened because Eleanor was reading. She read because I was the audience.

On this trip, Eleanor and I went on a horseback excursion up to Grinnell Glacier. Always adventurous both physically and mentally, Eleanor let herself be lowered with ropes over the top of the glacier down to a ledge below. So far so good! Unfortunately, she had a little more trouble coming back up. Upon being pulled up, her fingers were gouged on the ice. (I remember a lot of blood. But there was no permanent damage.)

Her prodigious artistic talent made her inventive and prophetic. In 1950, on the ceiling of my McLean Gardens apartment in Washington, DC, she projected marvelously fascinating color images, which swirled, changed, and evolved as we watched. Her tools were colored inks, placed on a slide with baking soda, and a slide projector. Catalyzed by the heat and light of the projector, a chemical process evolved before our eyes in gorgeous color and moving shapes, until it ended in an abstract image of unusual beauty. She displayed this "light art" to curators at both the Museum of Modern Art and the Guggenheim Museum.

In 1964, she gave a performance of this technique at the Museum of Modern Art in New York before an excited audience. Each performance was unique and composed on the spot. It was one of the first examples of performance art. It was so captivating for Eleanor that she asked, "Why paint?" However, she did eventually abandon it in favor of other art forms due to the impermanent nature of the medium.

There were always art materials around our house when I was growing up, and Eleanor was creating art there. I was free to play with clay in a bucket in the basement. Eleanor never

My painting "Ruth and Naomi." Now, I would call it "Sisters."

"taught" me, but I absorbed from her an openness towards self-expression.

She and I took trips to the sand dunes of Lake Michigan. Lying in the sand on starry nights, she introduced me to the cosmos: the Spiral Nebulae, the Milky Way, and Cassiopeia in her celestial chair. She introduced me to wonder and to awe.

Our lives were intertwined with art. In 1953 I made a painting that I called "Ruth and Naomi," based on the biblical characters from the Book of Ruth, not knowing I was unconsciously depicting Eleanor and me. In the Bible, Ruth tells her mother-in-law Naomi, "Where you go I will go, and where you stay I will stay." When a psychoanalyst friend saw my painting and said to me, "I didn't know you had a sister," I thought, "Of course, it is me and Eleanor."

Our shared world was full of hilarious laughter. Were we two peas in a pod? Were we twins born fourteen years apart?

I created a bronze sculpture that captured our close relationship. I call it "Playmates."

Her nickname for me was Mare, and mine for her was El. We had a tradition. Every year we made a gift for each other on our birthdays. Hers were touching, beautiful, often funny, and always memorable.

My sculpture "Playmates," circa 1985.

Here is one that I still have: It is a Styrofoam box covered in black lace. Inside are burnt-out flashbulbs that were used in cameras in that era, and a half-round of a silver cup with white lace, all reflected on a silver background. The somewhat magical, surreal image created on the reflective background is one of a throne, surrounded by chandeliers.

I love this piece as an example of her inventiveness and her ability to produce something quite perfect.

One of Eleanor's birthday gifts to me.

One of my birthday gifts to Eleanor.

On one of her birthdays, I made two small, connected clay pots with clay beads strung across the openings as a gift for her.

The inscription on the plaque reads:

> *El and Mare*
> *Two little cosmoses right and left*
> *Happy together like warp and weft*
> *See how they play, see how they dance*
> *Could you say they came together just by chance?*

In 1957, for my 45th birthday she wrote:

> *In endless space there are endless galaxies*
> *Each is a universe of awe*
> *There is one tiny microcosm that the senses can grasp*
> *That gives meaning to infinity: Mare.*

Eleanor eventually gave up some of her bohemian ways, married and had three sons, and had a successful art career. She and her family lived in Minneapolis.[1]

Harvey

Harvey was my handsome, kind, fun, heroic, larger-than-life brother. He was twenty years old when I was born. His nickname for me when I was little was "Buns" or "Little Buns." Later, he called me "Sis" and never patronized me. He was always there for me. I adored him, as did most women, children, and all dogs.

When Father died, I was 13 and he was 33. It fell to Harvey to take over the "pater familias" role. On a Sunday soon after Father died on January 17, 1926, I see Harvey ready to carve the roast, standing in front of Father's chair.

That he was of heroic proportions not only to me is attested to by his many accomplishments:

- College football All-Western Conference guard, playing on the University of Chicago championship team of 1913. (He was also the field goal kicker.)
- Lieutenant in the Tank Corps in World War I
- Successful businessman

My brother Harvey trimming his toenails with an axe on one of the annual fishing trips.

- Foreman during the construction of the then-largest earthen dam in the country on the Platte River in Nebraska

- Rancher in Colorado running 1,000 Hereford cattle each year on 13,000 acres of grassland

- A pioneer rainmaker who seeded the clouds in Colorado with silver iodine to literally make it rain.

One of Harvey's most formative experiences was serving in the Tank Corps in WW I. He served in the regular army first, as did my brother Francis, posted at Fort Sheridan. In 1917 he volunteered for the Tank Corps. I was taken to New York with Mother and Father to say goodbye and see Harvey off to France. The Tank Corps was brand new. It corresponded to the early days of the airplane, in terms of new technology, and it was very frightening to the enemy. Harvey signed up for that role, as he saw the tank corps as a "romantic" form of war service. He viewed the war as a game and an adventure, including his involvement in two major battles on the French front, at St. Mihiel and Meuse-Argonne.

In World War I, the commander of the tank, which he was, walked in front

Harvey in his WWI uniform.

of the tank and tapped messages to the driver. It is amazing that he survived. Harvey wrote many long and detailed letters home to the family from his war service France, and forty-six of these letters have been collected and published in a book entitled *The War As I Saw It: 1918 Letters of a Tank Corps Lieutenant.*[2] On his return from France, my family went to the Englewood train station on the south side of Chicago to meet him. Harvey was very thin, and he was suffering from trench mouth.

Upon his return from the War, he worked as the head of the housing department at Sears, Roebuck and Co. He left Sears Roebuck and Co. to serve as the foreman on construction of the Kingsley-Keystone Dam on the Platte River near Ogallala, Nebraska. Eleanor's husband Leo and his business partner secured the contract to construct the dam. At a certain point they had a dispute, and Harvey bought the tract of land in Colorado that became his ranch.

As a rancher in Colorado, he became interested in agricultural practices and artificial rainmaking through cloud seeding. He undertook the cloud seeding in conjunction with the Agricultural Department of Colorado State University in Fort Collins. My understanding is that he gave the University the use of some of his acreage for their experimentation with different kinds of grass seed and also with airplane spraying. I think the rainmaking may have been part of the same program.[3]

I have a post card that was addressed to Harvey from a nearby rancher expressing his gratitude for Harvey's success with the cloud seeding. It is addressed to Mr. Harvey Harris at Double Reverse H Ranch, Sterling, Colorado. It reads:

> *Dear Mr. Harris,*
> *We the people of the City of Fort Collins and all the farmers of Larimer and Weld County want to take time to thank you and yours for the wonderful and badly needed rain we got last night, May 16th. It saved us a lot of hard labor and headaches.*
> *Business is good in town today, too.*
> *Thank you again.*
> *Reno and all the farmers here*

Most vivid to me now is the image of Harvey on his horse "Tony," riding around his ranch mending fences and pulling wells. He pulled a lot of wells since the cattle had to have water at all times. There were windmills at each well.

Harvey married late and had no children, but every summer his ranch was summer camp for all of his nieces and nephews. One of the highlights was "dress-up day" at the ranch.

Harvey did not marry his first love, because she was Catholic and she insisted on his conversion. She never married, and when Harvey died she came to see Mother and brought a scrap-

Harvey and me, "dress-up day" at the Ranch, 1944.

book in which she had collected and kept many football newspaper clippings of him, and other memorabilia. She paid her condolence call and told Mother she would not be seeing her again.

Harvey and me.

Once when I was in Minneapolis visiting my sister Eleanor, Harvey was also there. We were setting off to visit Little Switzerland in nearby New Glarus, Wisconsin. Harvey drove, Eleanor beside him. I was in the back seat, experiencing pure bliss with my two favorite people in the whole wide world, my sister and brother. More than siblings, they were my spiritual parents.

"He was the finest man I ever met," pronounced the wife of his oldest friend. I agree.

Francis

I was not as close to my brother Francis, who was two years younger than Harvey. When I appeared in 1912, my two brothers were already in college at the University of Chicago. Francis was 18 years old.

I have vivid memories of my sisters in my earliest years, but my first actual memory of Francis was on my eighth birthday, when he gave me my beloved two-wheel bike. Experimenting in the ballroom on the third floor of our house, I soon learned to ride, and would ride around the neighborhood. That bike represented freedom to me. I am grateful to him for that first gift of freedom.

Francis was involved with photography from an early age. With his big box camera under a black cloth, he was the family photographer. (See page 8 for my one and only nude picture.)

As a twelve-year old reporter, editor and typist of a gazette, he gave his readers the intimate details of the family goings-on.

In the First World War, he and Harvey both volunteered at once, and both served overseas. Unfortunately, he was not made an officer, and spent his wartime as a cook in France.

I am sad when I think of him. I think he got a raw deal from the family. Harvey outshone him. Eleanor said Francis was the brightest of all of us, but his sharp and sardonic personality impeded him. He had a difficult life. He was in love with a Gentile girl, and my parents interfered, preventing him from marrying her. It was very sad. He did eventually marry someone else, and had two daughters.

Riding my bike.

When I was pregnant with my first child, there was a period when I was alone in Chicago. My husband Bernie had already moved to Washington, DC to start his job at the Board of Economic Warfare, and I was to join him after the baby was born. Mother was visiting brother Harvey in Colorado. Francis came and stayed with me (with his little bull dog) for a couple of weeks, and we had a nice time together.

From this vantage point, I look back and recognize how difficult it must have been for him to be the younger brother of the illustrious Harvey.

Francis in uniform.

Imogene

My sister Imogene (my oldest sister) was 16 when I was born. She and I were not particularly close. However, she appointed herself the official biographer and recorder of my baby book. This tome is a marvel. It relates the daily doings in my life as a baby with pictures, drawings, hair clippings, telegrams, cards, letters, plus who gave what baby gift. I have enjoyed it enormously and am very grateful to her.

Imogene

She was quite tall, with lovely blue eyes and a real musical gift. I see her in my mind's eye always at the piano. When I stop to listen, I hear Chopin or Debussy. She was well taught by the well-known Chicago teacher Glenn Dillard Gunn.

She was, I heard, a "sickly child." At her birth, a breech delivery, the doctor asked my father which one should be saved, the mother or the baby. Father must have chosen well, because they both survived. Mother was told she should not have any more children, but she had two more children after Imogene.

As a result of Imogene's health problems, I think Mother favored her. Imogene was sweet and docile, not a "holy terror," as Eleanor and I were sometimes referred to.

She got married in 1926 to Charles Kozminski, who came from a very well to do, rather famous family in Chicago. His father, Maurice Kozminski, was a Chevalier of the French Legion of Honor, and was the representative of a French Steamship Line. There was a public school on the south side of Chicago near us on 54th and Ellis Avenue that was named for him, the Kozminski School (now operating as the Kozminski Community Academy, still a Chicago public school).

Charles' family had been very well off prior to the depression. When Charles started to date Imogene, he came in a chauffeured car, and she was, I'm sure, dazzled. That all vanished with the stock market crash and the depression in 1929. They lost everything. Imogene, Charles, and their little

Kozminski Community Academy, at 54th and Ingleside Sts., Hyde Park, Chicago. Photo taken October 6, 2014.

boy moved in with us for many years. This had a major negative impact on my life, as Charles had many peculiarities that were very annoying to me.

Although I did not know it at the time, I am sure if he were alive today he would have been diagnosed with obsessive-compulsive disorder (OCD). I remember a few of his compulsions: In our library there was an oriental rug. When he entered the room, he had to walk the border carefully, and then he would sit down. But before he would sit down, when he came to his particular chair, he would swipe the bottom of the chair with his behind and then sit down. At the table, if we were having something like a roast beef, or something that had fat on it, he always wanted all the fat. He ate the fat, and he died, incidentally, at 54 or 56 of a massive heart attack.

His odd behaviors were so embarrassing to me that I did not want to bring my friends around. Imogene never talked to me about it, and she was ostensibly very faithful, but she suffered. She developed what the doctors suspected was Crohn's Disease. She gradually had most of her intestines cut out, and at one point she had a colostomy.

Imogene had a pretty happy life after Charles died. She got a job as a bookkeeper, and found much reward and satisfaction as a faithful volunteer at Passavant Memorial Hospital on Chicago's near north side. She had an apartment on the near north side and enjoyed her life. She died at age 74.

* * *

I was so fortunate that in addition to my parents and Aunt Annie, I had four older siblings who would do my bidding.

6

A SENSE OF PLACE

A Sense of Who You Are (and Who You Are Not)

Our Kenwood-Hyde Park Neighborhood

Our neighborhood on the south side of Chicago was called Kenwood. It was right next to Hyde Park. Hyde Park Boulevard was the separating line between Hyde Park and Kenwood, and we lived one block off of Hyde Park Boulevard. The school I went to, the Faulkner School for Girls, was also in Kenwood. One of my father's brothers, Sam Harris, and his wife and children lived right next door to us. Until the business dispute that led to the family split when I was twelve, there was a very easy relationship among the two families, almost like a single family.

Summertime in the neighborhood is very vivid in my memory. People sat out on their front porches until it got dark, and my cousin Sam (Junie) and I would play on the front lawn. The neighborhood children would gather and draw hopscotch boards on the blue-gray slate sidewalk with chalk. Hopscotch and the street game Ringolevio—which they called "New York," based on its place of origin—were the most popular games.

Being Jewish

Judaism, as a religion, played a very small role in my life. I went to Temple on the High Holy Days under protest. We did have Jewish dishes at meals at holiday time. I was confirmed at age twelve, but it had practically no meaning for me at the time.

Kenwood was not a predominantly Jewish neighborhood, but within the neighborhood there was a very tight-knit, insular Jewish community of which we were a part. Interestingly, the Jews did not associate with the non-Jews. It just didn't happen. There was a distinct separation.

My very good friend at the Faulkner School for Girls was Louise Greensfelder. She and I were very close, and were in the same class. Her father was a well-known Jewish surgeon. Her mother was not Jewish. When she got to be about 13, she was taken up by the non-Jewish girls in the class, and she became not Jewish. At that point, she changed her name to Toddy. And that was the end of our friendship. We never spoke about it. Years and years later, we met once for lunch at the Art Institute, and at the end of her life, we had a few letters of correspondence. But we never regained the closeness we had had.

I remember that during my freshman year at the University of Chicago, I was invited to a tea. My name, Marilee Harris, was not especially Jewish, so I think the people who invited me assumed I was not Jewish. I was so uncomfortable. I don't think anybody was ever verbally rude to me, but in a sense it was almost like being colored. You knew your place.

My parents had an experience of anti-Semitism in Wisconsin. They were traveling, and they were driving in a Pierce Arrow with a chauffer. They stopped at a hotel and the owner said, "We don't have any room. We might be able to put you up in back."

But Are You a German Jew?

In addition to the social separation of Jews and non-Jews, within the Jewish community there was a social hierarchy between German Jews and non-German Jews. If you were a German Jew, you belonged to a higher level of Jewish society. My friends at Faulkner were all the children of German families, and they would sometimes express this prejudice that they had heard at home against Eastern European Jews. When I would say "I'm not German, I'm Polish," they would say "But you're different. You're not like one of those kikes."

Another example of this bias is still very vivid to me. I was visiting my friend Rita Weil's family in Charlevoix, Michigan one summer, and we were sitting at the dinner table with the family. They usually spoke English when I was there, but among themselves they spoke German. They were speaking English at the dinner table, and then all of a sudden came the word "Ausländer." They were touching on something about Polish Jews or Eastern Eurpean Jews that would not have been nice, and then Mrs. Weil said something in German with the word "Ausländer," and the conversation was changed. She used the words "schweigen" and "Ausländer," meaning "Silence! We have a foreigner here." The foreigner (or outsider) was me, a non-German Jew. The German Jew bias against Eastern European Jew was very, very strong.

It was so strong, in fact, that when my cousin Mortimer, who grew up next door to me, married a German Jewish woman and had children, the children were led to believe that they were of German ancestry on both sides. When I met Mortimer's daughter, Jeanne Harris Hansell, my first-cousin-once-removed, in 1997 and told her about our Polish ancestors, she got a stricken look on her face. Not only was she shocked that this had been kept a secret in the family, but she was upset because it shook her identity of who she was. She, too, had grown up in Chicago with the bias against Eastern European Jews. The bias was within her own family.

The Family Schism

As is often the case with family businesses, a disagreement developed among the four Harris brothers in 1922 or 1923 about the best way forward for the business. Harris Brothers Company was evidently in some kind of financial difficulty, and my father had a different vision for the future of the business than did his three brothers. As treasurer of the company, my father did a lot of traveling back and forth to New York. He had established a connection with a bank there, and wanted to reorganize the company. His three brothers said, "You're taking the bread out of our children's mouths." He disagreed, pulled out of the company, started his own company, and that was the end of the relationship. It was also the end of what had been my experience of a large, extended, warm family group.

Father's leaving the company precipitated a sudden and complete estrangement from the rest of the family that I had grown up with—cousins, uncles and aunts. After that, I had no contact even with the cousins who lived right next door. I remember how awkward I felt living next door to my cousin Sam (Junie), who was my playmate from childhood, and suddenly not speaking to him and not knowing what to do. I felt terribly uncomfortable. Prior to the split, Junie and I, as children, played together all the time. I have a very distinct visual recollection of some members of my extended family sitting out on the front porch, in summertime, and Junie and I playfully fighting each other, rolling around on the grass in front. I remember going over there and playing in the hose and the sprinkler with him.

After the split, my father started a new business with my two brothers, called Frank Harris Son's Company. They rented office space in the McCormick building on Michigan Avenue in Chicago. Like Harris Brothers, it was a demolition and salvage company. They bought buildings and equipment from three World War I Army training bases—Camp Dix (now known as Fort Dix) in New Jersey, Camp Meade in Maryland, and Camp Grant in Rockford, Illinois—for demolition and resale. The company was only in business for two or three years before my father died in 1926.

Looking back on my life, I notice that the schism that resulted when my father pulled out of Harris Brothers Company was part of a pattern of family rifts that I experienced. Throughout my life there were numerous times when I felt anguish over torn loyalties. The first time was when my mother and my beloved nurse, Miss Stewart had a misunderstanding. The second time, as I have described above, was when I was about 11 or 12 years old and my father left the Harris Brothers Company, leading to the total rupture from the rest of the extended family that I had grown up with. The third time was when my brother Harvey and my sister Eleanor's husband had a business disagreement. The fourth was when my son and his father locked horns.

In all of these situations, I felt torn apart, and so became the peacemaker who didn't solve anything, but always had to "make nice nice" (as my daughter put it.) When I was in my 30's or 40's my mother said to me, "Why don't you stand up for yourself instead of letting everyone walk all over you?" I felt she was right, but what could I do about it? I did address this in therapy. Afterwards, my mother said, "I guess it's helped you, but you're not the same sweet girl you used to be." Damned if you do, damned of you don't!

My second husband, Bob Asher, commented jokingly on the family rifts saying, "Your family is more Sicilian than Jewish."

The Crime of the Century, Right in My Neighborhood

We lived on the corner of 50th and Ellis Avenue. Across the street from our house on Ellis Avenue was the Loeb family mansion. We played over there all the time. It had a tennis court in the rear, which became a skating rink in winter. The neighborhood kids were allowed to use both, and we did. Mr. Loeb was very generous to the neighborhood children. On Sundays, he would take a whole group of neighborhood children down to the drug store and buy them ice cream, including my sister Eleanor.

Their son, Richard Loeb, was known to all of us as "Dickie." My first knowledge of Dickie came when I was four or five, and my brother Francis bought a guinea pig for me from Dickie, who was raising them. (I didn't like it, and he returned it and got his money back.)

Bernie Shapiro, my first husband, who also lived in the neighborhood, was urged by his mother to play with Dickie while they were both in high school. "He's such a nice boy," she would say. Bernie received a gold watch chain from Dickie as a gift on his 18th birthday. My second husband, Bob Asher, was a friend of Dickie's, and their homes were contiguous to one another.

However, Dickie Loeb turned out to be not such a nice guy. Against the background of wealth, hospitality and kindness of his family, Dickie and his accomplice, Nathan Leopold, committed "the Crime of the Century," the vicious, brutal murder of a 14-year old neighborhood boy, Bobby Franks. Bobby lived up the street, on the corner of 51st and Ellis.

Dickie Loeb and Nathan Leopold decided that they would commit the perfect murder. They were bright young college graduates at the time, although only 18 and 19 years old. They planned a murder that they thought no one would ever discover. They decided that they would pick up a young boy walking home down Ellis Avenue from the Harvard School for Boys, which my cousin Sam (Junie) Harris and my second husband Bob Asher also attended. They were both on the list of potential victims. Pure chance saved them.

On that fateful day, May 21st, 1924, poor little Bobby Franks, who knew Dickie Loeb well, was walking home from school, and Leopold and Loeb offered him a ride in Leopold's car. He got in the car. They immediately murdered him. Then they took his body to the outskirts of Chicago and they stuffed his body in a sewer pipe and poured acid on him. They thought that this would make him unrecognizable.

CHICAGO HISTORICAL SOCIETY

Bobby Franks, the murder victim.

They planned to receive $10,000 in ransom money from a ransom letter they sent to Bobby Franks' family. They had packed clothes and rented a hotel room downtown for their getaway. They were going to go to Europe and have a fling.

However, the next day, a laborer saw a foot sticking out of a sewer pipe. It was Bobby Franks' body. Leopold and Loeb were caught, they were tried, they were convicted, but they were not hanged, because of Clarence Darrow's 12-hour defense speech. They got life in prison.

CHICAGO HISTORICAL SOCIETY

The scene where Bobby Franks' body was found.

This excerpt from the PBS website provides additional details:

> *Loeb…was obsessed with the idea of the perfect crime. His neighbor, a brilliant young man, Nathan Leopold, was a law student and a believer in Frederick Nietzsche's concept of the "superman"—the idea that it is possible to rise above good and evil. The two boys seemed an odd match. "Dickie" Loeb charmed everyone with his good looks and cool manner. Awkward-looking Nathan Leopold tended to hide in his friend's shadow. But the two young men formed a powerful bond. Nathan was in love with Richard and would do anything he wanted for sexual favors. He later wrote, "Loeb's friendship was necessary to me—terribly necessary." His motive for the murder, he said, "was to please Dick."*
>
> *Inspired by this odd mix of nihilistic philosophy, detective fiction, and misguided love, Leopold and Loeb hatched a plan to commit the "perfect crime." It was not so much the idea of murder that attracted them, but the idea of getting away with murder.*
>
> * * *
>
> *Leopold's and Loeb's parents hired the best, and most expensive, criminal attorney they could find—Clarence Darrow.*

* * *

The trial reached its climax with Clarence Darrow's argument,
delivered over twelve hours in a sweltering courtroom. Darrow admit-
ted the guilt of his clients, but argued that forces beyond their control
influenced their actions.... Darrow convinced the judge to spare his
clients. Leopold and Loeb received life in prison.

In 1936 Richard Loeb was killed in a prison fight with another
inmate. In 1958, after thirty-four years behind bars, Nathan Leopold
was released from prison. He died in 1971.

(PBS. "People & Events: The Leopold and Loeb Trial.")[1]

The case took over the newspapers. Tourist buses would drive up and
down Ellis Avenue to point out the Loeb residence and the Franks' house.
(They still do today.) I was kept in the house quite a bit at that time because
of all the buses coming up and down the street.

Everybody was up in arms about the fact that someone with that background—wealthy, Jewish—would commit such a heinous crime. Even more
shocking was the fact that Bobby Franks and Dickie Loeb were distant
cousins, and had played tennis together on the Loeb family courts many
times.

Before Leopold and Loeb were arrested, there was speculation in the
media that two teachers from the Harvard School of Boys may have been
the murderers. Bob Asher, my second husband, was president of the freshman class at the Harvard School for Boys, of which Bobby Franks was a
member. The police and the newspapers called Bob at the time to talk to
him about the case. Here is what Bob recounted of his experience, in an
interview he did with the Association for Diplomatic Studies and Training
Foreign Affairs Oral History Project, in November 2000:

I was the class president that freshman year and therefore got
involved very early in the case as a good friend of Bobby Franks, who
at first appeared to have been kidnapped for ransom. I knew Dick
Loeb, and my sister was in a birding class led by Nathan Leopold....
[On that] Wednesday, when I got home from my dentist appoint-

ment, I got a call from Mrs. Franks asking whether I knew where her son was. He was normally home by that time. It was 5:30, six o'clock. I said I didn't know because I had left school at three o'clock ... and had gone downtown to the dentist. But I would try to find out for her. And I established the fact that he left school around 3:30, as far as anyone knew, walking south from 47th Street to his home on 51st Street, and should presumably have been home by the time she had called.

...[H]e had been picked up by Loeb and Leopold in their car. They were looking for any eligible young person of the group that they knew at Harvard School, including, as they later said, Junie (Sam) Harris, me, Johnny Coleman, Bobby Franks. They really weren't particular. But Bobby Franks came along at the right time, apparently with a tennis racket in hand, and they said they wanted to see him and his racket. He took the ride and it cost him his life. Smashed on the head. They later tried to extract a ransom and it was some days before they were actually caught.

Meanwhile, they had written a ransom note on a typewriter, and I was asked to find out what kind of typewriters we had at school. I was interviewed by the police. That really taught me a lesson I have never forgotten, because I was taken down to the central office and they would say to me, "Now, your gym teacher, was he a friendly man?" And I would say, thinking I was being kind, "Oh, yes, very friendly." "Would he ever put his arm around you?" "Oh, yes. If you struck out or fumbled a ball or something, he would put his arm around you and tell you it was okay." "Get that gym teacher down here for questioning," said the police officer, thinking my comment might prove a homosexual relationship.

Then he said, "Your manual training teacher, was he friendly?" And I said, "Oh, yes, he would go out with us on Halloween and our parents were satisfied that we were under some kind of control...." "Get that manual training teacher down here!" And pretty soon I began to wake up to the fact that I was going to have the whole faculty in jail unless I shut up. So I became more discreet, after they started questioning me also about our male English teacher.

But the lesson it taught me was that just by virtue of being questioned, these innocent people had things brought out in the newspapers...that marked them for life. If they had had a divorce, it raised questions in some quarters about should they be teaching, that sort of thing. And what I learned was, be careful what you say when you are being grilled.

In my neighborhood, our backyard almost touched the Loeb's tennis court. We thought this was wonderful because Dick Loeb and his siblings had been instructed that, if there were other kids in the neighborhood who were playing on the Loeb court, they didn't have the right to send them home, they had to wait their turn. This was supposed to be evidence of how well brought up they were, but obviously, something went wrong. It may have been in letting them go through school too quickly.

I was a pall bearer at Bobby Franks' funeral.... My recollection is that Dick Loeb was at the funeral, an innocent looking neighborhood friend. There was a big turn-out from the neighborhood.

(Asher and Kennedy, ASTD, 2001.)[2]

The former Loeb residence as it looks today, on Ellis Avenue, Chicago. Photo taken October 6, 2014.

So, my husband Bob was quite involved in the aftermath of the murder. And, he was very lucky that he had a dental appointment after school on May 21, 1924.

After Loeb and Leopold had been arrested but before they had been convicted, a skull and crossbones appeared on the doorstep of our house, and a message that said "If the court don't hang them, we will" and signed "K.K.K." They mistook our house for the Loeb house, which was across the street. It was meant for the Loeb house.

Our normally quiet Kenwood neighborhood was roiled by this brutal, lurid, and sensationalist event.

Today, the Kenwood neighborhood has the leafy green appearance of a suburban community, with large homes and well-tended yards. On the previous page is a photo of what the former Loeb house looks like today.

A few blocks away stands the Chicago home of President and Michelle Obama.

GREWSOME SYMBOL OF DEATH IS LEFT NEAR HOME OF LOEB

(Picture on back page.)

A human head, a pair of withered arms, and a single discolored leg—placed in the form of the piratical skull-and-crossbones symbol — were found opposite Richard Loeb's home last night as a grewsome reminder of the morbid interest that the Franks murder trial has aroused.

Caught between the elbows of the two arms was an envelope addressed to: "Chicago, City of Crime." Enclosed was a piece of white paper on which had been printed this sinister and ungrammatical warning:

"If the court don't hang them, we will. K. K. K."

The symbol of death rested on the porch of the Frank Harris home at 5000 Ellis avenue, across the street from the handsome Loeb residence.

Harris is president of the general merchandising firm of Frank Harris Sons company, 332 South Michigan avenue. He is the uncle of Samuel H. Harris Jr., living next door, who was one of the boys selected by the youthful slayers as a probable victim of their experiment in crime.

FAMILY AT WHOSE HOME GREWSOME THREAT WAS LEFT. Family of Frank Harris on steps of their residence at 5000 Ellis avenue. The cross shows where a dismembered human body and a theatening letter was left.
[TRIBUNE Photo.]   *(Story on page two.)*

Article and photo that appeared in the **Chicago Daily Tribune,** *August 19, 1924.*

7

HUSBANDS AND CHILDREN

"These Are My Jewels"

I have two children who are currently the center, the interest, the worry, the pleasure, the "raison d'être" of my life.

Bernie and I had waited to have children until America entered World War II, because we were worried about bringing Jewish children into the world if Hitler were to invade the U.S. We were not that sure of victory in the beginning. Other friends felt the same way, and waited to start their families until after it was clear that America would be standing up to Hitler.

My son Harvey, age 16.

On January 19th, 1943, towards evening, it began to snow. I had every reason to suspect that an occasional cramp could mean that my already late baby was on the move. So my sister Eleanor and I packed up cards and games to amuse us through a long wait and, in a Chicago blizzard, we arrived at the Michael Reese Hospital about ten PM. However, there was no time for games. Harvey Harris Shapiro (named after my beloved brother Harvey) was born on the cusp of midnight, January 20th, 1943. This changed my life forever.

He arrived 7 lbs. 8 ounces, fully armed and ready to go. When our pediatrician first held him to be fluoroscoped (X-rayed) at three months, the vigorous and loud protests caused the doctor to observe, "You'll never have another one like this!" Prophetic!

A case in point: One day in McLean Gardens, where we lived on the first floor, my upstairs neighbor reported that Harvey (then aged 5) called me loudly: "Mother. Mother. Mother!" Receiving no answer, he yelled "GOD-DAMMIT MARILEE!" He never took life lightly.

Harvey at his desk.

After surviving his adolescent years, he fulfilled his father's dreams. He was elected to Phi Beta Kappa and won a Woodrow Wilson scholarship in his senior year at Reed College. Instead of pursuing English Literature, his major, he became a doctor and then a psychiatrist. There are hundreds of patients who owe him much. He paid his dues. Harvey's son Jacob, who lives in California, is my only grandchild.

My daughter Joan, at age 16.

Aside from his support and devotion to me, more than any parent would hope for, I have in Harvey a true friend.

Six years later our much wished-for daughter, Joan Lettie, arrived. During the afternoon of February 11, 1949 my Mother, who was visiting us in Washington, DC, and I went downtown to see the movie "Hamlet" starring Lawrence Olivier. I am somewhat ashamed to say that I had never read or seen the play prior to that. It bowled me over with emotion and excitement, so that the twinges in my thighs did not register for what they were.

Joan Lettie Shapiro was born at 8 AM on February 12, 1949. Not only was she born on Lincoln's birthday, but the moon was full. Auspicious! The nursery nurse at the hospital informed me that the nursery was full to over-flowing. She added that the doctors don't believe that more babies are born on full moons, but the nurses know it to be true because it always happens, without fail. Observation trumps "science!"

Another preordained fact was that my dearly loved Aunt Lettie, Mother's youngest sister, offered a diamond bracelet in exchange for our naming our daughter after her. A done deal. Add to this that when Joan was about two and a half, my mother said to me, "This child will be a great comfort to you."

Does being like a third leg, or a personal memory pad, or a fashion arbiter and personal shopper, make for comfort? Absolutely. And add her inborn radar about people, her unerring eye for structure and color, and her hilarious humor. Even though sometimes she might put on her hard hat of street smarts to cover her generous, soft, warm, and empathetic heart, we are not fooled.

Joan and her father, Bernie Shapiro.

Her life has become one of service. And her creation of unique and beautiful bead necklaces is an expression of her innate artistic talent. She claims to be channeling her aunt Eleanor, my artist sister. My mother called it right when she said Joan would be a comfort to me. She is also a true friend, and for that I am so grateful.

From time to time I have wondered what life for me might have been like without children. Never to have fully participated in "the banquet of life," to have missed fulfilling the part we are meant to play… unthinkable!

In ancient Rome, Julia, a noble matron, was asked to show her jewels. Pointing to her children she said, "These are my jewels!" Well said, Julia!

My Husbands

I married two men. Sequentially, of course. God love 'em both. I certainly did.

They shared a common suffering when they married me. Bernie soon learned that brassieres hang on doorknobs and that toothpaste tubes assume quirky shapes and often lose their little hats.

Bernie Shapiro sparkled like the tail end of a meteor as it streaks across the sky. He was brilliant, full of fun, and played the violin rapturously and with the skill of a professional. He was a Doctor of Jurisprudence, in other words a J.D., and was sometimes referred to as a lawyer's lawyer. Life was never dull with someone as gifted as Bernie was.

Smarty Went to a Party

On February 9, 1935, my first best friend, Charlotte Klein, had a party to celebrate obtaining her Master's degree in social work. I wore what we then called a "Sunday night dress" (although the party was not on a Sunday or in the evening). It was long, tight, brown and low-necked. There I met Bernie Shapiro. We danced and drank a bit.

After a week or so, Bernie asked me to go out with him, his sister Zelda, and a male friend she had met on shipboard coming home from a visit with her sister in Palestine. His name was Marcel Wagner, a Frenchman who lived in Alexandria, Egypt. It was an evening of destiny.

Then followed a whirlwind of dates with Bernie. We often rode horseback together. Bernie had joined the ROTC in college so that he could ride. He was on the polo team at the University of Chicago, and a perk was free horses on weekends.

On Saturday nights we dressed up and danced at the Balloon Room of the Congress Hotel, where we ate Dover Sole Marguery for $5.

We both knew, early on, that this was going somewhere. Bernie had landed a job with a very prestigious Chicago law firm, Taylor, Miller, Busch and Boyden. He was earning $250 a month, while most of his law school friends were earning $25.00 a week. He was 29 years old and ready to get married. I was 22 and more than ready to be rescued from my job with the emergency relief agency.

Bernie was an eminently eligible bachelor. After a couple of months we told Mother we wanted to get married. She was pleased to give her blessing after her only question—"Is there any insanity in your family?"—was answered in the negative.

We had two weddings. Early on our wedding day we went to the home of an orthodox Rabbi (this was important to Bernie's mother) who married us under the traditional "Chuppah." Then, to seal the deal, with two more Rabbis jointly officiating, we married again at our home on Ellis Avenue with our immediate families present.

I came down the grand staircase of our house on the arm of my brother Harvey, to the strains of Mendelssohn's glorious "Midsummer Night's Dream" march, played on the piano by Bernie's Aunt Birdie.

In the library, the two Rabbis and Bernie were waiting. The ceremony began, led by Rabbi Levi. The aged Rabbi Stolz, who had married my parents, started the Benediction and, midway through, forgot the prayer. Bernie, well versed in Jewish lore, prompted him. We got through the ceremony, and finished with the traditional stomping and shattering of the wine glass under foot.

The lunch and leave-taking are a blur to me. I do remember vividly, however, that when we reached the city limits, I unpinned my orchid corsage and with "I guess I won't need this anymore," threw it out of the window. Since I can't recall Bernie's reaction, I must conclude it rendered him speechless.

Our French friend Marcel Wagner played a singularly important role in our lives. After Bernie's and my first date at which Marcel had been present, he told Bernie, "She is the girl for you. She has a beautiful left shoulder and dancing legs. Anyone can have a beautiful right shoulder, but a left one is special." This made no sense to me, but evidentally it was persuasive. Four months later he sent us a case of "Old Ancestor" Scotch for a wedding present. It cost us $100.00 duty to collect it.

Marcel's sophistication, worldliness, charm, and the exotic world in which he traveled and did business fascinated us. He would remonstrate "The Sphinx has been there for four thousand years. Why are you Americans always rushing?" He might start the day with a pink gin. He had business in Chicago. One mission was to buy "a nest" of Duesenberg cars for the Shah of Iran and one for his Queen. The American Eastern Company was his firm, and it was involved with shipping through the Suez Canal. He was very rich, and lived with his wife and four children in Gstaad, Switzerland. Marcel Wagner became our dear friend who taught us so much about the world, and when we were together, we were all *bon vivants*.

Honeymoon

On a spectacular, moonlit night, on the deck of our ship to Bermuda, conversation turned to wonder about the moon and the stars. To my surprise, I found that my Doctor of Jurisprudence didn't even know that the moon revolved around the earth. Horrors! Did the surprise that I felt at this gaffe somewhat balance the shock he had felt when I threw the corsage out of the car window?

But there was more to come. It was our first night in the dining room of our elegant hotel, and, in evening dress, I ordered a salami sandwich. Bernie was embarrassed, but I assured him that "if you were to the manor born," then you could order what you liked. His reply was, "Did you mean manor or manure?" This was a good example of his wit and the earthy, fun relationship we had together.

Things Not To Do (Notes for a Bride)
- Hang your brassiere on a door knob
- Forget to screw the toothpaste cap on tightly
- Store the Limburger cheese in the Fridge
- Use garlic or pepper on food
- Throw your wedding bouquet out of the car window

Time to Sell the House on Ellis Avenue

It was 1936. The Depression had lightened. My sister Imogene and her husband Charles got back on their feet, and they moved to their own apartment. Our house needed to be sold, since Mother could not live in it alone. The plan became for Bernie and me to move back into the house with Mother temporarily while we put the house on the market for sale.

A couple were hired to help. William and Mary were perfect. She was gentle, sweet, and a good cook. William, the essence of a movie-type butler, not only kept the furnace stoked with coal, but put on his white coat to serve dinner. He also shined Bernie's shoes.

One morning at breakfast Mother looked up from her paper and asked Bernie, "where exactly are the Bahamas?" He replied, using the Yiddish word *beheymus* which means a clumsy, oafish person, "You should know. You have most of them in your family." Mother threw her napkin in his face! (Not the usual mother-in-law and son-in-law relationship!)

Bernie and me on Skyline Drive, 1948.

As a couple we fit seamlessly into the family. Those pre-war years were wonderful. There were seven of them. Then nature intervened. Mary got pregnant and gave birth to a girl she named Marilee. Never again to enjoy such household peace, we ultimately moved, and the house was closed. I vividly recall my mother, on our last night in the house, leaning against the mantle over the fireplace and weeping. She had lived in the house for over 40 years. The house was eventually sold for "peanuts."

In our first apartment at the Mayfair at 56th Street and Hyde Park Boulevard in Chicago, a few things stand out. I was not prepared to be a grown-up householder. I did not know how to operate a vacuum cleaner, or that a carpet sweeper could be opened to remove what it had picked up. As for cooking, I made fudge, but I had to ask Bernie "just how do you boil an egg?"

"Your place looks like a goat's nest," said my friend Rita Pfaelzer on her first visit. We laughed then, but my lack of proper training only made things harder.

Going downtown on the streetcar in Chicago (the fare was six cents) in my stunning nutria-skirted winter coat, I was an anomaly. I was not comfortable. I felt conspicuous and out of place, because I was so elegantly dressed and looked so different from the other riders. Not only the coat, but my long black hair and my too-large nose did not blend well with all those broad-faces with blonde hair.

I associate these images with my first pregnancy, which ended in miscarriage. It was a boy. I never appreciated the loss until now. Who was he?

My Hound Dog

Vicky came to us through a dog-fancier friend. She was a black and white spotted English setter. She was overweight, sweet, docile, and a true neurotic if ever I saw one. I loved her anyway.

She occasionally had what seemed to be fainting spells. She would lie on her back, eyes rolled back, tongue hanging out to one side. I would cover her gently and soon she would come around. (A psycho?)

She didn't like the rain, and would only take care of her functions if Bernie held an umbrella over her. She snored so loudly that she had to sleep in a closet at night.

We had two friends in our apartment building who were doctors at the prestigious Michael Reese Hospital. Vicky developed an unsightly cyst on her lower jaw. Our friends arranged for its removal at the hospital.

Sadly, the owner of our apartment building wanted our apartment for his own use. He used our innocent Vicky as an excuse to evict us. We had difficulty finding housing that would accept dogs. A friend who had a farm offered to give Vicky a home. Her disappearance from their farm was never accounted for.

Before and After Pearl Harbor

Our next apartment on 46th Street between Greenwood and Woodlawn in Chicago was a building that housed a political spectrum of tenants.

On the third floor there was a couple named Rachmiel and Esther Levine. Rachmiel Levine was a doctor who later became quite well known because he did ground-breaking research on how insulin transports sugars in the body. He and his wife Esther were communists. On our door and on the door of neighbors across the hall were posters "There will Always Be An England!" Rachmiel and Esther had to go past these posters on their way to the third floor. An uneasy social relationship resulted.

I recall listening to Rachmiel expound on the current situation in Europe. I was really very innocent about politics, and I would listen to Rachmiel, and he knew exactly what was happening, and why, and what to do about it. I remember saying to my husband in all sincerity, "Does President Roosevelt know what Rachmiel knows?"

One day, after hearing the news on the radio, I called out through the window to Esther as she approached the apartment entranceway, "Hitler has marched into Russia!" She kept on walking, replying, "I'll believe it when I hear it on my own radio station."

Making the rounds in the building on a New Year's Eve, we went upstairs to call on the Levines. It was a mistake. The assembled group became instantly silent when we arrived. We did not stay.

In 1942, Bernie applied for a job with the Board of Economic Warfare in Washington, DC. He needed an FBI clearance for the job, and the FBI came and talked with our neighbors, asking them questions about Bernie. The FBI knocked on Esther's door to inquire about Bernie, asking "Does he have any Communist leanings?" she replied, "That damn capitalist?!" and she closed the door. Bernie received an unusually quick clearance for his new job with the Board of Economic Warfare! She once said to Bernie, "I'm sorry I ever met you, because I like you and you're a capitalist."

We learned later that Esther had died in childbirth. Rachmiel went on to do research and made an important contribution in the treatment of diabetes. An excerpt from his obituary that appeared in the *New York Times* on March 1, 1998 describes his work, and his exceptional cognitive and critical thinking abilities:

Dr. Rachmiel Levine, whose experiments on how insulin increases the body's use of blood sugars overturned conventional scientific belief and set new courses for diabetes research, died on Feb. 22 in Faulkner Hospital in Boston. He was 87 and lived in Newton, Mass.

* * *

Dr. Levine was skeptical of explanations that held that insulin needed to enter the cell to turn on enzymes there. Instead, he reasoned that insulin worked on the outside of the cell to stimulate the transport of glucose and other sugars. He set out to obtain proof in experiments using dogs at Michael Reese Hospital in Chicago.... Dr. Levine's findings were so accurate that four decades of subsequent insulin research using sophisticated methods have proved him correct, said Dr. Jesse Roth of the Johns Hopkins University School of Medicine.

The standard explanation of how the transport mechanism works is known as the Levine effect, and it opened up subsequent work on how hormones modify cell functions.

* * *

His results showed that insulin was like a key that unlocked the cell membrane, allowing the sugars to get inside.

* * *

"He could unify a lot of diverse thinking into clarity," Dr. Gorden said. "Dr. Levine was one of the great thinkers in the biomedical community. He helped resolve many complex issues."

In 1978, under Dr. Levine, a team at City of Hope, along with scientists at Genentech Inc., produced human insulin from recombinant D.N.A., the first time a human hormone had been synthesized in a one-celled organism.

Born in Zaleszczyki, Poland, (a town now in Ukraine) he received a bachelor of arts degree from McGill University in Montreal and a medical degree from McGill Medical School in 1936.

He worked at Michael Reese Hospital and New York Medical College before he became executive medical director at City of Hope in 1971. He became deputy director for research emeritus in 1984.

Dr. Levine was a member of the National Academy of Sciences. He was president of the American Diabetes Association from 1964 to 1965 and of the International Diabetes Foundation from 1967 to 1970."

(Burkhart, *New York Times* 1998)[1]

After Pearl Harbor everything changed. I became pregnant. Bernie left for a job in Washington, DC with the Board of Economic Warfare in September 1942. In April 1943, I arrived with our three-month old son Harvey in Washington, DC to at last be reunited with Bernie in his tiny apartment on New Hampshire Avenue, just off Dupont Circle. We were evicted in the first week. No dogs or children were allowed. So we moved to Lee Gardens, in Virginia. This apartment was a third-floor walkup without air conditioning. I remember boiling diapers and bottles there in July and August.

We moved again.

There was a village called McLean Gardens, right in the middle of the Northwest section of Washington, D.C., that had been built to house government workers and military personnel. It had been the estate of Evelyn Walsh McLean, of Hope Diamond fame. Residents came from every state in the Union. They were families plunked down in Washington for the duration of the war. We were among the lucky ones to get an apartment there. Bernie bet the manager $100 that he could not find us an apartment. Fortunately Bernie lost.

By day there were buggies and playgrounds and kids running around safely outdoors. By night alcohol was the social currency and common denominator. Our small two-bedroom apartment was frequently the scene of last minute cocktail parties. Scotch and soda, crackers and salami (with or without cheese) were *de rigueur* in hundreds of evenings of conversation with our friends. There were frequent lunches with my women artist friends at which we drank Sherry mixed half and half with dry Vermouth and shared gossip.

The guests were a diverse crowd. There could be a wounded veteran, someone who worked at the government's Lend Lease Program office or the OPA (Office of Price Administration), others from Bernie's own agency—the BEW (Board of Economic Warfare)—or neighbors who did not work for the government.

But there was also the sad and infuriating reality of living in wartime. We would hear that somebody was missing in action, or a convoy ship carrying desperately needed cargo had been torpedoed.

As the war ended, the BEW became the U.S. Commercial Company (USCC). In 1947 Bernie went to Japan for the USCC to help re-establish the Japanese cultured pearl industry. The cultured pearl is begun artificially by placing a tiny piece of shell in an oyster. This foreign bit is gradually coated by natural processes in the animal until it becomes a pearl. The pearl beds in the sea are tended and harvested by divers. In the course of his negotiations he met with General Douglas MacArthur.

While on this mission, he stayed at the famous Imperial Hotel in Tokyo, which was designed by Frank Lloyd Wright. Young women from some of the most important families of Tokyo staffed the housekeeping. They worked there because they were hungry, and they were able to get food at the hotel after the long war years. Their unfailing Japanese graciousness and courtesy dazzled Bernie. Upon entering his room, they bowed first to him, and then again to the photograph of his 4-year old son. One day he told them he was having a lady visitor in the afternoon. When he came into his room he found the bed carefully turned down.

After Bernie left government service in 1948, he went into private law practice. Looking back, Bernie said the best years of his career were when he was with the government.

Airplanes

For years, I would not fly. I turned down trips to the Argentine, and to Europe with Bernie who was going on business (and it would have been first class, expenses paid), because I was afraid to fly. I still don't believe it can work!

I was 42 when I took my first airplane flight. My brother Harvey died and I had to fly to attend the funeral in Chicago. The stewardess held my hand. I was terrified. But I discovered that a scotch and soda allayed my fears quite nicely.

But I never could relax on a plane. I used to be amazed when I would see people get on the plane, sit down and open a book while I was sitting there so tense. I did get a little more comfortable with it, but I still listen for any changes in engine sounds and other signs of potential trouble.

Humor Helps

Sometime around 1952, in a discussion about dependency with my psychiatrist, it was suggested that my wearing beautiful, expensive hand-me-downs from my sister Eleanor was a contributing factor to my dependency on others. Sadly, I wrote this to Eleanor, who lived in Minneapolis. Soon after, I got a letter from my brother-in-law Leo. He said that they were sorry to hear what the psychiatrist said, because a box containing some Dior originals was wrapped and ready to be sent to me.

My ever-resourceful husband, Bernie, shot back a telegram: "Fired the doctor. Send the box!"

P.L. Travers Comes to Dinner

We had some very good friends, Arthur and Emily Gardner. Arthur Gardner worked at the state department, and Bernie and he became friends through the negotiations their two agencies had. It was April, and I believe the year was 1973. The Gardners were coming for dinner—just the two of them. They called and asked if they could bring an out-of-town guest. I said, "Of course." Their guest turned out to be Pamela Travers, the Australian author of Mary Poppins. She was at that time, I think, 73 years old. She was evidently an old friend of the Gardners and was their houseguest.

She was very, very nice and just a lovely person. She was not stylish one bit. I recall that she was plump. The one thing that I remember that she talked about at some length was the word "crone," the word for an old woman. The word "crone" she said, is derived from the word "crown," and is really meant to signify the crowning wisdom of old age. But its meaning has been perverted into a negative thing.

She and I shared an interest in the Gurdjieff work. Pamela Travers' (née Helen Goff) interest in esoteric philosophies, mythology, and spirituality are mentioned in the biography of her written by Linda Cranston:

> When she finished school Pamela worked briefly in an office. She was also a poet, a journalist and an actress. She changed her name to Pamela Lyndon Travers as her acting career advanced. In 1924 she emigrated to England and concentrated on a writing career, becoming known as P. L. Travers.

Life in England

Very soon after her arrival in England Pamela found success as a writer. Some of her work was published in the Irish Statesman, whose editor was the poet George Russell. Russell wrote with the pseudonym Æ or A.E.

Æ was a theosophist and introduced Pamela to this esoteric philosophy. Under Russell's influence Pamela also became very interested in spiritualism and mysticism. In addition, Russell introduced Pamela to William Butler Yeats, an Irish poet, and to Irish folklore. Pamela was already fascinated by fantasy before she met Russell, and found Irish myths to be a rich source of inspiration. Russell was known for his kindness towards younger writers and remained friends with Pamela until his death in 1935.

Pamela's intense interest in myths and hidden meanings stayed with her throughout her life. She spent some time studying with George Gurdjieff, a spiritual teacher, and also stayed with a Navajo Indian tribe in the United States. She said that they gave her a secret name which she promised never to reveal.

(Crampton, 2004.)[2]

Her archived papers in the State Library of New South Wales, Australia reveal that:

> the 1964 Disney film version of Mary Poppins…stimulated wider public interest in P L Travers and her work. It is from this time that articles by Travers about her work began to appear in magazines and journals. She received invitations to lecture in the United States and was Writer in Residence at Radcliffe Hall, Harvard University (1965–1966) and at Smith College (1966). Travers made frequent visits to the United States where she lived during World War II, and from 1969 until 1977.

(Anemaat, 1991.)[3]

Her visit was memorable, because she was memorable. She wrote me a lovely thank you letter, and that was the only contact I had with her. The letter was mailed from Grand Central Station in New York, and has a New York City return address on it, so she must have been living in New York at that time.

Her letter reads:

> Dear Marilee Shapiro,
>> Here is the little monograph I promised you.
> I hope you like it. Pass it on to Hugh Ripman.
>> It was so nice seeing you again. And I liked
> meeting Joan and reading her poems.
>> I hope we will meet again.
>> Thank you for a delicious dinner.
>>> Yours sincerely,
>>> Pamela Travers

The thank you letter I received from P. L. Travers.

I'm sure she is mistaken about saying she was seeing me again. I only met her once.

My marriage to Bernie was full of fun and laughter, and also some darker days. Today, at age one-hundred-and-two and looking back, it is a blur of raising children, training dogs, car-pooling, trips both wonderful and not so great, of successes, losses, high moments, and despair. It was not dull. I was married to Bernie Shapiro for thirty-nine years. It was the best of marriages and, at times, the worst of marriages. In other words, it was a quite typical marriage.

In 1974, when Bernie was sixty-nine, he suffered a massive heart attack. He survived for seven months. I am grateful for that time, which allowed the innocence and simplicity of our early years to come alive again.

Do You Remember Me?

Sometime in the early 1980's I got a phone call. "Do you remember me?" the caller asked. It was Robert Asher. Of course I remembered Robert Asher from our childhood days in Chicago. We had grown up in Chicago one block from each other, and gone to the same University High School, and the University of Chicago. "Well, my wife and I are now the proud possessors of one of your ceramic lamps," he said. He and his wife had also moved from Chicago to Washington, DC. He explained that his wife had insisted that he see the lamp before she purchased it, and when he turned it over, there was the signature "Marilee." Surprised, he said to his wife, "I know her."

Several years later, Bob's wife died. I was away and only discovered it in our U High Bulletin on my return. I wrote him a condolence note, which he answered with a telephone call. We spoke of shared memories. He recalled his first encounter with me—a summer day long ago, when he had gone to play with his best friend, my cousin (and next-door neighbor) Sam "Junie" Harris. When he arrived, he saw a little girl in a bathing suit running through a sprinkler on the front lawn of his friend's house. Junie immediately said to Bob, "This is my cousin Marilee; she is going home." While they threw their ball back and forth, ignoring her, she sat on the curb pretending not to care. She had black hair and an unusual name. She was eight years old.

He recounted this memory to me in 1987, when I was 75, and he was 77. I was not surprised a few weeks later when he called again, suggesting dinner. When I opened the door in my favorite yellow Mexican dress he said, "You look great." We began dating.

When Bob first came to call, my boots were beside the entrance, twisted in a wrong relationship to each other. Immediately, he bent down to right the wrong, right boot right, and left boot left. I also never learned to load the dishwasher the "right way," and after dinner the pots and pans and general disarray were incomprehensible to him. However, none of this darkened our comfortable companionship, our shared observations, and almost perfect compatibility. He was rare, a complete human being.

We dated for 6 years, and then got married in 1993. Our shared educational experiences and our common background enriched our relationship, and similar perceptions of the past and the future were an exciting discovery. For instance, Bob had switched from the Harvard School for Boys in Chicago, which offered a very traditional, classical education (similar

Bob at the Grand Canyon, 1988.

to the one I received at the Faulkner School for Girls), to the University of Chicago High School in tenth grade. I had made a similar switch in 11th grade. (We were not at U. High at the same time, as Bob was two years older than I.) Bob, in the interview with the Association for Diplomatic Studies and Training, describes the same cultural shift I experienced in transitioning from one school to the other:

> *[John Dewey's] educational philosophy was to interest the students and then proceed, deepening and widening their interests, so that if you had music ability or wanted to learn more about instruments, musicians, and so on, you were encouraged to do so at the University High School. You were discouraged at Harvard (School for Boys), because arithmetic and grammar and geography were considered basic and more important, and you could worry about your music later.... It [University High School] was easier I thought, as far as demands on the students were concerned, because they didn't require as much homework and compulsory courses.... The University High School was liberating in a sense. It had clubs of all kinds: a Writers Club, a French Club, an Engineering Club.... I was graduated at the top of the class of 125 and I don't think I worked half as hard as I did when I was in grammar school, but I had a wonderful time.*

(Asher and Kennedy, ASTD, 2001.)[4]

Bob had an illustrious career, although it started out humbly. Right after college, he was a volunteer organizer with the League for Industrial Democracy and Chicago Workers' Committee on Unemployment, and an aspiring writer. His first published article, entitled "The Jobless Help Themselves: A Lesson From Chicago" was published in *The New Republic* in 1933. The New Deal was just beginning.

After getting a Master's degree in public administration, he got a job with the American Public Welfare Association in Chicago for $25 a week. His life changed dramatically when, in 1934, his boss there received a call from Harry Hopkins of the new Roosevelt administration, asking him to recommend someone for a job in Washington.

Bob was selected and left immediately for a six-week job in Washington with the Federal Emergency Relief Administration. After this assignment ended, he worked for the WPA (Works Progress Administration), which helped artists, writers, musicians, and actors who were destitute during the great depression. He met Mrs. Roosevelt, who was interested in their work

Bob and me at the exhibit of my mother's artwork at the Hyde Park Art Center in Chicago in 1995.

investigating whether they could provide some income for residents of Appalachia who were in dire poverty by selling their handmade crafts.

After WW II began, he went to Algeria with the Lend-Lease Administration, which had established a civilian supply program in North Africa. Under the auspices of the Allied Force Headquarters and the Lend-Lease program, he lived in Algiers, working to bring in supplies for the civilians (pharmaceuticals, textiles, materials for making shipping crates, etc) "to prevent disease and unrest behind the lines."[5]

In January of 1944, he began working for the United Nations Relief and Rehabilitation Administration (UNRRA) and was involved in the repatriation of displaced persons, slave-camp laborers, and prisoners of war. He had the honor of representing UNRRA at the ceremonies in Paris for the repatriation of the millionth Frenchman on June 1st, 1945, only three weeks after VE day.

After UNRRA's functions were taken over by the U.N. High Commissioner for Refugees, he was offered a job by the State Department as a member of the U.S. Resident Delegation to the Economic Commission for Europe, based first in London in 1946 and 1947, and then in Geneva from 1947 to 1950. While working for the Economic Commission for Europe, he attended meetings in Paris on the formation of the Marshall Plan, along with the country directors for all the 16 countries involved in the Marshall Plan. He moved back to Washington in 1950 to work in the State Department's European Bureau.

The last nineteen years of his career were spent with The Brookings Institute. During this period, Bob and Edward Mason, Dean of the Graduate School of Public Administration at Harvard, were asked by the World Bank to co-write the history of the first twenty-five years of the World Bank. Their book, "The World Bank Since Bretton Woods," has turned out to be a very valued and an important work.

Of course, all of this took place before we began dating. Bob and I had twenty-one years of wonderful companionship together, until he passed away in 2008 at age 98, five days before his 99th birthday. Bob Asher was twenty-four carat gold. I can think of no virtue that was not his. He was the soul of decency, intelligence, honesty and generosity.

8

ART RUNS THROUGH IT

I awoke to contemporary art in the nineteen thirties, when I first saw the paintings of Picasso at the Art Institute of Chicago. Picasso's work resonated with me in a way I had never experienced. I felt a sense of recognition, and an intense emotional response. The first quarter of the twentieth century is my time, and I have never fully left it behind. I believe no one ever truly leaves the time slot into which one was born. From the WPA art class where I got my first introduction to sculpture, through painting, drawing, etching—even digital art—the ideas, shapes, and manner of expression of those early years have shaped what I do artistically.

When I was about 24, I bought some plasticene, a clay-like material that never hardens, and began to experiment with it. A simpering piece of three maidens holding a garland of flowers that I created was placed on the mantle of a doting aunt's fireplace. This encouraged me.

My enjoyment of the work with plasticene led to the discovery in 1937 of a WPA (Works Progress Administration) class in sculpture in a nearby public school basement. The WPA was a large-scale program initiated in 1935 by the federal government under President Franklin D. Roosevelt that gave work to millions of Americans who were unemployed as a result of the Great Depression. According to Wikipedia, the WPA funded the construction of 40,000 new and 85,000 improved buildings and infrastructure projects including "roads, bridges, schools, courthouses, hospitals, sidewalks, waterworks, post-offices ... swimming pools, parks, community centers, playgrounds, coliseums, markets, fairgrounds, tennis courts, zoos, botanical gardens, auditoriums, waterfronts, city halls, gyms, and university unions. Most of these are still in use today."[1]

In addition, a project funded under the WPA called Federal Project Number One "employed musicians, artists, writers, actors and directors in large arts, drama, media, and literacy projects."[2] The enormous contribution of the WPA can be seen today in the beautiful murals and sculptures decorating post offices and other buildings around the country that were made by individuals who went on to become important artists.

Unlike my piano studies, my experience sculpting with clay was not reading notes on a page to translate to keys on a piano. Working with clay meant placing your fingers into the very stuff that is you. Home at last!

Sculpture is tactile, sensuous, and kinesthetic. Words like "body," "primal," and "primitive" come to mind. When one is sculpting, the center of gravity is in the pelvis. One's feelings seem to come from the gut, or the root chakra.

I took this WPA class for two years. The teacher was a young Italian man named Arturo Fallico. The enthusiasm in his teaching was inspirational. Later, Arturo earned a Ph.D. in aesthetics, and wrote a book on aesthetics called "Art & Existentialism." He also taught philosophy at the University of California.

Around this time, the famous sculptor Alexander Archipenko came to Chicago and opened his teaching studio, the Modern School of Fine Arts and Practical Design. Archipenko is most renowned for his Cubist-inspired sculptural style. The Encyclopedia Britannica provides a concise description of his sculptural style:

> He began to explore the interplay between interlocking voids and solids and between convex and concave surfaces, forming a sculptural equivalent to Cubist paintings' overlapping planes and, in the process, revolutionizing modern sculpture. In his bronze sculpture *Walking Woman* (1912), for example, he pierced holes in the face and torso of the figure and substituted concavities for the convexities of the lower legs. The abstract shapes of his works have a monumentality and rhythmic movement that also reflect contemporary interest in the arts of Africa.
>
> (Encyclopedia Britannica, "Alexander Archipenko.")[3]

Archipenko took a circuitous route to Chicago. He was born in Kiev, Ukraine in 1887, which at the time was part of the Russian Empire.

After studying in Kiev, in 1908 Archipenko briefly attended the École des Beaux-Arts in Paris, but he quickly abandoned formal studies to become part of more radical circles, especially the Cubist movement.

(Encyclopedia Britannica, "Alexander Archipenko.")[4]

In 1912, Archipenko…opened the first of his many art schools, joined the Section d'Or group, which included Georges Braque, Marcel Duchamp, Fernand Léger, and Pablo Picasso, among others, and produced his first painted reliefs, the Sculpto-Peintures.

* * *

In 1923, he moved from Berlin to the United States, where over the years he opened art schools in New York City; Woodstock, New York; Los Angeles; and Chicago…. For the next 30 years, he taught throughout the United States at art schools and universities, including the short-lived New Bauhaus. He became a United States citizen in 1928.

(Guggenheim Museum Collections, "Alexander Archipenko.")[5]

"Walking Woman" by Alexander Archipenko; Bronze, 1912.

What good fortune that he accepted me as one of his students! He was a great teacher of few words. We always worked from the nude model. I learned how to handle the techniques of working with clay: how to hollow and prepare for firing, various finishing techniques, and above all, what makes a form finished and good. I worked with him for two years.

In 1938 I had my first gallery show. It was a two-person show with my sculptor friend Kate Goldberg, at the Paul Theobald Gallery.

In 1940 I studied with the Chicago painter Rudolph Weisenborn. I used charcoal, and was very much influenced by cubism in my drawings. For some reason Weisenborn thought my work was funny. I took this as a compliment.

This was a rich period of learning for me: of going to galleries and museums, discovering the art world. Archipenko exhibited some of his students' work in a New York City gallery, and mine was one of them. I began to feel like an artist.

My first sculpture exhibit, Chicago 1938, with Kate Goldberg (left).

Then came Pearl Harbor. Bernie went off to Washington to work for the Government, and my son, Harvey was born. By 1945, I was living in Washington, DC and ready to become an artist again.

The Artists' Guild in Washington, DC was formed during World War II. It was originally a group of local artists that got together and asked, "What can we do for the war effort?" I don't know that they did anything for the war effort, but it was a way for artists to support each other, to meet and talk, and to exchange ideas. It was a select group, and you had to be voted in. I don't remember who sponsored me, but I was voted in after the war had ended. We met at members' homes.

There were wonderful opportunities to exhibit at that time in Washington. There were group shows at the Smithsonian, at the Corcoran, at the Baltimore Museum, at the Art's Club. These were juried shows that everybody submitted to. There was a lot going on among the local artists. However, I was aware that women artists had an uphill battle. Sexism in the art world was very prevalent, but unrecognized.

I remember one episode that is so typical of what happens between older artists and younger artists. (Now, at age 102, I'm one of the old ones and I have sympathy for what was going on then.) But back then, I was one of the young ones. The Guild was having a show, and I submitted what was probably a pretty crappy piece, but it was experimental. It was plaster figures attached to some heavy wire screening that is used in construction, and then put into a frame.

Prentiss Taylor, who was an accomplished, first-class printmaker, illustrator, and painter, and the president of the Artists' Guild from 1943 to 1950[6], objected to my piece. He said, "This is not worthy of the Guild." So I, thinking of my right to freedom of speech, said, "You can't do this to me. I have a right to show it." Eventually, the piece was shown, and I think later went into the garbage can, because it really was not good. I was defending my right to free expression. I was a young upstart artist, and the conservative, staid, real artist objected—rightfully so.

When I think back on this episode, I am embarrassed about it. Now I see myself on the side that Prentiss Taylor was on, doing a bit of judging of the work of younger artists. I see some work that is so bad I just can't believe it!

Parenthetically, Prentiss Taylor had a very distinguished career not only as an artist, but also as an art therapist. When Taylor worked as an art therapist, one of his clients was Ezra Pound, along with his wife and son. He published an article entitled "Art as Psychotherapy" in the *Journal of American Psychiatry* in 1950. Although he was white, Prentiss Taylor was close to many of the influential figures in the

The poster for our two-women show in Chicago, 1940.

Harlem Renaissance, such as Langston Hughes, singer Jimmy Daniels, and writer Carl Van Vechten.[7] Taylor was also romantically involved for a time with Aaron Copland, the composer of Appalachian Spring.[8]

The Artists' Guild held annual shows at the Corcoran Gallery for a number of years, starting in 1943. Here is a review from the *Washington Post* of the second annual Artists' Guild show at the Corcoran Gallery in 1944:

Throng of Friendly Visitors Sees Washington Artists' Guild Exhibit

A large and friendly throng of visitors more concerned than usual on these occasions with looking about the room as well as at each other, turned out for the opening of the second annual exhibit of the Artists' Guild of Washington at Corcoran last Sunday.

What they saw was a display ranging from the solidly conservative to the experimental, a varied assemblage that contains work of real distinction, has plenty of verve to carry it over the weak spots, and that marks a positive gain over last year.

This gain is more significant than it would be in normal times. Without bothering to mention the fact that a good part of the vital creative talent in this country is now channeled in other directions, there is a certain type of aesthetic defeatist who has taken the moment to proclaim (as one did in a recent magazine article) that "American art, like American literature, seems to be in retreat." Since the airing of this view is prevalent and goes with a tendency to burrow underground for the duration, it is a pleasure to report any evidence to the contrary.

Gallery Is Full

The show at the Corcoran, which consists of close to 100 entries in all, is composed of paintings, sculptures, prints, and drawings. The gallery is full to capacity and in some places the hanging had to be doubled. Several sales have already resulted, including works by Paul Arlt, William Calfee, Sarah Baker, and Edward Rosenfeld, the last named exhibiting with this group for the first time.

Since portraits, except for the slick variety, are in the minority these days, it is worth noting that there are several completely unaffected and able paintings in this category. Carl Nyquist's portrait of an Irishman is the best work by him that we have ever seen, and we liked the forth-

right yet sensitive character of the two contributions by Sybil Bonbright. One of the surprises in the show is a spirited oil by the printmaker and water colorist, Prentiss Taylor, the first, he says, in about 18 years.

The only war subjects offered are by two members, Olin Dows and Mitchell Jamieson, who have been on active service with the Army and Navy respectively. Examples of commissioned work by these two, who are well known to Washington, were lent to the exhibit by the Government.

Work Characteristic

In addition there are several nonmilitary paintings and sketches by members of the Guild who are now serving with some branch of the service. These include a vertical figure painting by Jack Berkman, landscapes by Sheffield Kagy and Robert Gates, and drawings by Kenneth Stubbs.

The majority of the exhibitors have shown here frequently, and most of them are represented by characteristic work, some to better advantage than others. The Corcoran teachers, Richard Lahey and Eugen Weisz, for example, are both represented. Andrea Pietro Zerega has a typical landscape and a more ambitious, not too successful, figure study, and Walter T. Carnelli, an arresting self-portrait and a landscape previously shown here. Harold Giese has one particulary successful small oil, and there is an excellent pair by Oke Nordgren. Several of the women painters have contributed still lifes.

(Watson, *Washington Post*, 1944.) [9]

[Author's note: Typographical errors that were in the original text were retained.]

The Artist's Guild continued from the War until sometime in the '50s, and then it just kind of died away.

When I first came to Washington, there was a gallery called The White Gallery that was then taken over by Franz Bader. The Franz Bader Gallery became the most important gallery, and probably the only one at that time that exhibited contemporary art. It was a gallery and a wonderful bookstore combined.

At that time I was already interested in Zen, and would look for books on the topic when I would come in. Franz, knowing of my interest, would say, "Oh, there's the *meshugganah* shelf," pointing to a particular bookshelf. Which meant, "There's the shelf that would have the kind of crazy stuff that you're interested in." I got a kick out of him saying the "*meshugganah* shelf."

Bill Calfee, a sculptor, had a studio school on "U" Street in Washington, and I began to work with him. He was a great teacher and became a lifelong friend. With him I expanded my understanding of aesthetics and the world of contemporary art.

Sculpture was always my focus, but I did begin to branch out. I was still young in art in 1945, and new ideas and techniques excited me. I had been working in our McLean Gardens apartment. I experimented with holding a candle eight inches below a piece of

One of my "smoke technique" watercolors.

paper clipped to a board, which would leave a trail of candle smoke on the paper. Or, a paper pressed against random drops of paint on a surface would yield blotches to be read like a Rorschach test. When I did these experiments while sipping a glass of sherry and listening to my favorite music, I saw wondrous things in the smoke marks on the paper. I painted them with watercolor, and these paintings became the works exhibited in my first one-person show at the Watkins Gallery of American University.

This show came about as a result of a real dressing-down I received one day from Bill Calfee. "You have talent but no guts," he said. I was crushed, and decided to show him my drawings. He liked these, and as a result he offered me that one-person show at the Watkins Gallery in 1947.

These years were exhilarating. Bill had become chairman of the Art Department at American University, and we felt the art world's ferment and excitement. Young GI's just out of the army enrolled, and young and up-coming artists such as Jack Tworkov and Tony Smith visited. I had my own cubicle workspace at American University, and spent three productive years in that environment.

The Phillips Gallery was a museum like no other. It had been a private home, and as a gallery it was a place where one could visit, relax in any of the rooms, smoke a cigarette with ashtrays provided, or read undisturbed while drinking in the marvelous paintings on the walls. Around 1975, there was a young Chinese artist, Yuen Yuey Chin, who gave a class in classical calligraphy at the Phillips Gallery, and I enrolled. It was exotic, fascinating and difficult. To obtain proficiency would require devotion and concentra-tion beyond what most Westerners are willing to give. Accustomed to having music in my studio while I worked (mostly Mozart and Beethoven) I found this totally incompatible with the practice of calligraphy. This was a perfect example of culture clash.

While spending a summer vacation in Maine, I took a course in begin-ning etching and found it exciting. On my return to Washington I found a class at a First World War building then known as the Torpedo Factory, which was turned into an art gallery. After a while I thought I had learned enough to have my own etching press. That was a mistake. Being alone with my press, I found that I missed the atmosphere of a common workplace and the stimulus of other people. That was too important. I sold the press.

Delving Into My Unconscious

During the period that I was making the watercolors with the candle-smoke–on-paper technique, I consulted a psychiatrist about of the behavior of my six-year-old child. The doctor said to me, "I always start with the mother." So began my endless road to self-knowledge.

I began to meet and fear my unconscious. I remember making a sculp-ture of a hollow skull with a pearl in an empty eye socket. It felt scary, like something dark and mysterious. I couldn't let it control me. I stopped the "trickery" of the wine and smoke. I stopped being able to do what I had been doing artistically. I felt something devilish was producing these images, not me. Some force was at work—it might be witchcraft, it might be evil forces. I glimpsed the relationship between these dark images and my fears, and fortunately was able to bring those dark things to light. The occult, black magic, witchcraft, has never bothered me since.

Except once: Sixty years after I felt that the dark forces that had once scared me were gone for good, my imagination entrapped me once again. It was pitch dark, in the middle of the night. I felt a gentle breeze on my face. It came again, and began to waft past me at small regular intervals. I tried to figure it out. It continued in utter silence. I became uneasy. It continued. Then the thought of Salem witchcraft came to me out of nowhere. The breeze continued now in clockwork punctuality. Now aroused and in full alarm mode, I woke my husband. He turned on the lights, picked up the wastebasket and caught the bat.

At an exhibition at Gallery Plan B, Washington, DC, 2008.

But back when I was struggling to free myself from the dark forces lurking inside me, I said to my doctor one day, "You have made me happier, but you have ruined me as an artist." This angered him and he brought his fist down on the desk with an emphatic "NO! NOT TRUE!"

And it's not true. But it did change me. In therapy, I learned to identify the images I was using in drawing and painting and sculpture, and what they stood for in my psyche. Once you know what it is, it doesn't have mystery anymore. It reduces the spontaneity of the creative process. This is both a negative thing—a loss—and a positive thing, allowing the possibility of growing in aesthetic terms. My impulse to create an image, regardless of the medium, did not come from my head. Once having analyzed this impulse in therapy, there was a loss of innocence. I became more sophisticated about myself, and in my artistic technique, resulting in more "finished" works. However, I think my earlier works are better because they are more raw and emotional.

At the Faulkner School for Girls, there had been a great emphasis on Greek mythology, and this has been a big influence in my life, particularly in my art. The Greek myths also influenced me psychologically, because all those goddesses and gods represent parts of the human psyche. I was happily doing sculptures, not knowing what I was doing from a psychoanalytic point of view; but my sculptures were related, all of them, to the Greek myths. I've done Venus, for instance, which is a torso without a head. And I've depicted Daphne, the nymph that was chased by Apollo and turned into a tree, over and over and over again.

When I was creating these sculptures, I was thinking of the nymph, Daphne, but not knowing that what she stood for applied to me—to my confused feelings about sex. Apollo was chasing after her. She called to her father, Peneus, the river God, to save her from Apollo's clutches. He changed her into the Laurel tree.

Another myth I depicted in my art many times is that of Europa and the bull. Zeus changed himself into a bull and kidnapped Europa, a woman. Again and again, I've done the bull, with the woman on the bull.

Associated Artists Gallery

In 1960, Dorothy Goldberg and I decided to start a gallery in the coach house belonging to The Phillips Gallery. Until then, it was used as a studio by multiple artists. The coach house stood on the ground that now is the parking lot of the Cosmos Club. We invited Lillian Goldman, a painter, and Harvey Moore, a sculptor and bronze caster to be our partners. We called it the Associated Artists Gallery. Stealing from Jackson Pollock, Lillian and I dribbled gallons of multi-colored paint over the gallery floor, which was a great success at the opening.

Shortly after we opened, Dorothy's husband, Arthur Goldberg, was appointed Secretary of Labor in President Kennedy's cabinet. This changed everything. Suddenly we made the front page of the style section of *The Washington Post* almost daily.

Dorothy was inventive. She instituted a

Deep in thought in front of one of my sculptures at a show at the Associated Artists Gallery 1960.

bag-lunch program at which slide shows and discussions took place. She arranged a show of the paintings of Henry Miller, the very controversial writer whose books such as *The Tropic of Cancer* were banned in this country. The titles of some of his paintings included sexual allusions, words not used in polite conversation that were not familiar to some of us and had to be defined.

In 1960, Associated Artists Gallery gave an homage show to the Barnett Aden Gallery, which was the first privately owned black gallery in the United States.[10] Despite the fact that all of these things we did were trend-setting, our gallery was short lived. Dorothy had to quit because of her new position as the Labor Secretary's wife, we lost our lease, and after only two years we closed.

My Experience as an Art Therapist

"Purchase order." That was what I was at the National Institute of Mental Health (NIMH) for a period in the late 1970's when I worked there as an art therapist on a research study after Bernie died. I was in my late 60's. I had been a student of art therapist Elinor Ulman, and she recommended me for the job. I became assistant to Hanna Kwiatkowskia, who was a founder of family art therapy. The focus of the study was adolescents from middle class families who had dropped out of school. Mostly all were involved with drugs.

Before treatment began, the patient and his/her whole family were required to participate as a family in an art session. They were each given an easel, colored chalks, and paper, and asked to draw themselves. Another exercise was to draw the whole family at the dinner table (including grandparents if they were living with the family.) A final request was a joint picture in which they decided on the theme of the picture and produced it together.

A box of Kleenex was also provided, in case of tears, which were frequent.

The session was videotaped for later staff discussion. Remarkably and invariably, the tentative diagnosis from the art session was corroborated in the talk therapy with the psychiatrist.

Subsequently, I taught students of art therapy enrolled at George Washington University who needed to learn techniques in handling clay. I provided private classes in my studio.

An example of my work in my new digital medium. "Amaryllis," 2012.

Going Digital at Age 88

As I moved into my late eighties, physically lifting large, heavy sculptures became out of the question for me. I needed a new medium to carry me into my declining years. When I was eighty-eight years old in the year 2000, I registered at the Corcoran School of Art for a class called "Introduction to Digital Art."

I was totally unfamiliar with computers. I was at least 60 years older than my classmates. I learned very little in that class. Fortunately, my instructor, himself an artist and printmaker, agreed to be my private tutor in Photoshop. I can now work with digital images on the computer, adding an exciting new dimension to my work. I sometimes feel like a genie, because touching one button turns green to blue. Touching another button enables me to move a portion of what is on my screen to another place on the screen.

I continue to make smaller sculptures in bronze and steel. However, tired of repeating images from my own inner landscape, I am currently taking lessons in photography for a digital camera. I very likely won't live to amortize my expenditure, but I don't care. It is a worthwhile challenge.

The Creative Process

I used to think that suffering was needed to produce art. While I am very familiar with the frustrations of the creative process, a successful result gives me pure joy. The dialogue that occurs between me and the piece I am work-

At work in my home studio, August 2014. I am currently doing a series of smaller sculptures exploring the shape of an egg.

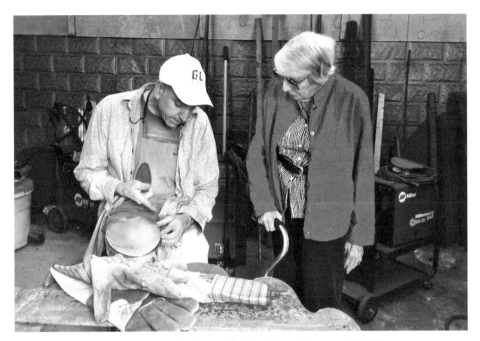

A recent piece of mine being worked on at the foundry in Lovettsville, VA. With Mike Clay, foundry owner.

ing on does not always go my way. The material can say "no" to me and then I must listen and find another way to reach my goal. This is the creative process.

I have no personal philosophy of art. I do it because there is nothing else I would rather be doing. In the studio, with an ongoing project in which I am absorbed, time does not exist. If I stopped to think about it, I would have to say that I am happy.

So, here I am, a century old. By some odd act of grace or luck I am still able to make reasonably small sculptures and work with the computer. Looking back, would I have rather been doing something else? I think not. The making of an object of art, the creative process, is a struggle. It involves all of one's attention and intuitive powers. For me, it has been fascinating, joyful and totally life-enhancing. This struggle, this pursuit of a vision or an idea, is what I have always loved to do.

9

MY JOURNEY TOWARDS WHOLENESS

My sister Eleanor once said to me, "We were born for more pagan shores." Our bohemian and artistic interests did not neatly fit into the restrictive and conventional society into which we were born.

It seems to have been my lot in life to be "one of them" rather than "one of us." It began when I was six years old at the Faulkner School in Chicago at Christmas time. All that beauty of a tree ornamented gorgeously, the music, the lovely stories— they weren't mine. I am Jewish. I felt like an outsider throughout my childhood, and into much of my adult life. I felt that I didn't belong.

Much later, during the years in which I was an exhibiting sculptor, I was always interested in esoteric

A birthday gift Eleanor made for me: a whimsical sculpture of the two of us.

ideas. I dabbled in Zen, studied etching and Chinese calligraphy, took lessons in Flamenco dancing and, at age fifty, became seriously interested in the Gurdjieff work (a philosophy and set of spiritual teachings, explained below.) I became a member of a Gurdjieff group in Washington. After several years in this group, a remarkable thing happened to me. I became aware that I belonged, that they accepted me, no matter what or who I was. No longer "one of them," I became "one of us."

Our season's greetings card, 1957.

First, Zen

One Sunday morning in the mid 1950's, I heard a new, exotic book entitled *Zen and the Art of Archery* reviewed on the radio while I was carpet sweeping. Bernie had taken the children to Sunday school, so I was alone. It was fascinating, and I became excited. I was hearing things I seemed to already know. But how come that Japanese guy who wrote the book knew it, too? It was quite a mystery to me.

I got the book, which was a seminal book in the beginnings of the Zen movement in this country. So began a period of my voraciously reading anything I could find on the subject of Zen. There wasn't much, though, as translations were just starting to become available in bookstores. The West Coast was ahead of us. I heard of Zen retreats going on in California. For me, this was an intriguing but scary possibility. Could I hack it? How to act? What to pack? Do you bring your eye makeup? I never attended one.

During this period, Daisatz Suzuki, the renowned Japanese Buddhist scholar, gave a lecture in Washington. In a front row seat, I drank in his words, and for twenty-four hours after his talk I was transformed! His very presence inspired me. Of all the disciplines and spiritual paths, I still think that one, for me, is the most enticing.

I began to talk about my interest in Zen with artist friends. In the fall of 1962, I received a letter from Peter Blanc, an artist friend living in New York. We had had adjacent studios when we were art students at American University in 1948. There, our discussions covered art, various philosophies including Yoga and Zen. Peter wrote that there was a person in Washington with whom I could "further my studies." He put me in touch with Hugh Ripman, who was the leader of the Gurdjieff group in Washington, D.C.

"The Work"

I was 50 when I met the Gurdjieff work. On the morning of Thanksgiving that year, 1962, I went to meet Hugh Ripman at his home in Washington. Two vivid impressions hit me upon entering. First, the smell of a turkey roasting, and, second (and more importantly), my immediate recognition of this man. "I think we may have met at a parent-teacher meeting some-where," I said, "or at some other place?" He said no to all the possibilities, and yet I knew that face.

We talked about my interests and which books I valued. He said that there would be a Gurdjieff group starting to meet in January 1963. It would be "a group of stray dogs," as he put it. The only requirement would be that one be disillusioned with life as it was.

So began years of Monday night Gurdjieff group meetings, which soon became important enough to be inviolate. More than once, Bernie and I were invited to go to the Kennedy Center or out to dinner on a Monday night, and I would not accept because of my commitment to the Gurdjieff group. Which meant that poor Bernie was deprived, and I regret that today.

The journey of self-discovery based on the ideas espoused by Mr. Gurdjieff has been my second education. It is called "The Work."

"The Work" is based on the teachings of George Ivanovich Gurdjieff, a philosopher and spiritual teacher who was born in Armenia in 1866.[1] Gurdjieff was concerned with the question of humanity's place in the universe, and the search for the meaning of life on earth. He wanted to know the answers to the questions "Who am I?" and "Why am I here?"[2]

I'm sure most of the readers of this book will not be familiar with Gurdjieff, so here is a little background from Wikipedia:

> *George Ivanovich Gurdjieff (January 13, 1866–October 29, 1949)…*
> *was an influential spiritual teacher of the early to mid-20th century*
> *who taught that most humans live their lives in a state of hypnotic*
> *"waking sleep," but that it is possible to transcend to a higher state of*
> *consciousness and achieve full human potential. Gurdjieff developed a*
> *method for doing so, calling his discipline "The Work" (connoting*
> *"work on oneself") or "the Method." According to his principles and*
> *instructions, Gurdjieff's method for awakening one's consciousness is*
> *different from that of the fakir, monk or yogi, so his discipline is also*
> *called (originally) the "Fourth Way."*
>
> *In early adulthood, Gurdjieff's curiosity led him to travel to Central*
> *Asia, Egypt, India, Tibet and Rome, before returning to Russia for a few*
> *years in 1912.*
>
> *The Work is in essence a training in the development of conscious-*
> *ness. During his lifetime Gurdjieff used a number of different methods*
> *and materials, including meetings, music, movements (sacred dance),*
> *writings, lectures, and innovative forms of group and individual work.*
> *Part of the function of these various methods was to undermine and*
> *undo the ingrained habit patterns of the mind and bring about*
> *moments of insight.[3]*

Gurdjieff had a very creative, imaginative, science fiction way of explaining the meaning of life on Earth. It was a parable. It was very complicated, and I can't say that I completely understood it. For a long, long time, I didn't understand it. But then, as I looked at it, I saw that it correlates surprisingly well with how things are. One of his very interesting ideas was that life on Earth is an experiment, and it may not work. And there are some ways that one can help out individually. What one can do is to become more conscious of what one is and what one does, especially in relation to other people. And in so doing, one finds release from the habitual obstacles that our own personality makes for us. In revealing these obstacles, opening them up and dealing with them, we find release from them. The correspondence of this to psychotherapy is very close.

I learned to separate out and understand parts of myself that were obnoxious and to temper them. I also learned that I am not alone—that everyone has difficult and negative characteristics and acts accordingly. While these characteristics cannot be eradicated, they can be ameliorated so that one is no longer a puppet to one's habitual ways.

"Night and Day," a recent work of mine.

It involves self-examination, looking inward at our own dramas and our own issues, how we relate to other people in the world, and really examining it closely. And we do this examining in the presence of, and with the help of, a group of people that we come to be very familiar with, because we meet with them every week. There is also some meditation involved in the Gurdjieff work.

One of the precepts, which is very psychological—I don't think this necessarily came from Gurdjieff, but this became very important—was the concept of many "I"s, many people in me. The identification of who, in me, is feeling this way, is a very important concept. More than just "the child" in me and "the adult" in me, there is the snobbish me, the defensive me, etc. There are many "I"s, and it is helpful to name them. To become aware of the "I" that is speaking for all of me is to be able to control it. So, my children learned to say to me when I got upset with them, "Remember your nice self."

The Gurdjieff work became, and remains today, an integral part of my life. It was freeing to discover that one's secret fears and frailties are present in everybody else.

I was already deeply familiar with the esoteric teachings of Buddhism, Hinduism, and Taoism from reading about them, but this was different. This was the application of some of these ideas to my life as I lived it.

As I mentioned, in traditional psychotherapy I learned what the images I was using in my artwork represented in my psyche. The Gurdjieff work showed me the role they play in my habitual responses. Through the Gurdjieff work, one develops control over one's responses by practicing having a different response. It involves changing one's sense of perspective on life itself, and a change of values.

I've been involved in "The Work" for 51 years. I still find it meaningful and helpful, and I still attend weekly Monday evening meetings. My friends there—my "Work" friends—are very important to me. Not from a socializing standpoint, because this is not where socializing takes place. But because our relationship is so deep, and based on such understanding.

To have encountered "The Work," and to have been able to take in the inner meanings, has been my great good fortune. I believe nothing else could have changed the course of my life so deeply, quietly, and powerfully. I credit "The Work" with helping me reach my present age of 102. Looking back at the struggles and pleasures of 102 years, I would be willing to do it again.

The "merry chase" continues…

ADDENDUM

THE FAMILY BUSINESS:
DEMOLITION, SALVAGE, AND RE-USE

My grandfather, Moses Harris, founded along with his four sons the Chicago House Wrecking Company, a salvage company in Chicago that "specialized in demolishing buildings and then selling the building materials and contents to the general public."[1] A successor company, the Harris Brothers Company, was a huge catalog mail-order company that sold everything under the sun. My father was the treasurer for these companies from the time the Chicago House Wrecking Company was incorporated in 1893 until 1922 or 1923, when he left to form his own salvage company.

My nephew, Leo J. (John) Harris, has done extensive research on the Chicago House Wrecking Company and Harris Brothers Company. John (the youngest son of my beloved sister Eleanor) is the family historian, and has had several articles published in magazines that recount the remarkable accomplishments of these companies. I'm going to let him tell a lot of the story. He writes of my grandfather:

> *Moses Harris (1840-1900), a Russian immigrant who was variously described in Chicago city directories during the 1870's as a peddler or junk dealer in rags and used metals, was eventually to earn his living by salvaging, recycling, and selling building materials and related memorabilia obtained from dismantling world's fairs, expositions, and other monumental public and private structures. By the end of his life, Harris had gone from a simple scrounger of rags and scrap metal to become a sophisticated and well-to-do huckster of pre-owned materials. Moses Harris and his four sons, Abraham, Frank, Samuel, and David, were surely among the earliest conservationists, long before that term was to have any meaning to the general public.... [T]he officers of the Chicago*

House Wrecking Company believed that they were 'engaged in the saving and utilizations of property, much of which would be otherwise absolutely wasted.'

(Leo J. Harris, 1999 and Samuel H. Harris, 1908.)[2]

The Chicago House Wrecking Company dismantled the Chicago World's Fair in 1894 (officially called the World's Columbian Exposition at Chicago), as well as three other World's Fairs:

- The 1898 Trans-Mississippi Exposition at Omaha
- The 1901 Pan-American Exposition at Buffalo
- The 1904 Louisiana Purchase Exposition at St. Louis

John notes: "The Company would sell the materials so salvaged at either the fair sites, or from its office and yards in Chicago, or by mail order. During the first twenty years of its existence the Company issued over 170 multi-page catalogues for that purpose."[3]

In 1900, my father, Frank Harris, went to Paris to bid on the Parisian World's Fair on behalf of the Chicago House Wrecking Company. They did not get that contract.

The Ferris Wheel at the World's Columbian Exposition at Chicago, 1893.

The Chicago House Wrecking Company purchased the huge Ferris Wheel that had been at the 1893 Chicago World's Fair. They took it to the Louisiana Purchase Exposition at St. Louis and operated it there in 1904, before taking it down and selling the parts for scrap.

John discovered that:

The Ferris Wheel, built and operated by George W. C. Ferris, had a glorious history at the 1893 World's Columbian Exposition in Chicago. In the season beginning June 21, 1893, it carried nearly 2,000,000 people in its 36 cars, each capable of containing 60 persons and an attendant, on a ride that lasted 20 minutes. The wheel itself had a diameter of 250 feet, its axle weighed 70 tons, while the entire apparatus weighed over 4,200 tons.... It took 175 freight cars for the Chicago House Wrecking Company to move the dismantled Ferris Wheel from Chicago to St. Louis for the Louisiana Purchase Exposition.... Operating the Ferris Wheel required 44 persons, including guards, platform guides, an engineer, and a fireman. The boiler required four tons of coal for each day's operations.

(Leo J. Harris, 2011.)[4]

The Chicago House Wrecking Company did not dismantle only World's Fairs and Expositions. The company also dismantled a number of major buildings, structures and infrastructure systems, both public and private, including

...the U.S. Custom House and Post Office in Chicago; the Old Bay View Mills of the Illinois Steel Company in Milwaukee; the Four Seasons Hotel at Harrowgate, Tennessee; the old Post Office, Weddell House, and the Case Building in Cleveland; and the old cable street-car system in Chicago. For variety, the company also salvaged steamships that had foundered on the shores of the Great Lakes. From just one steamship, the company obtained 4,000,000 pounds of barbed and fence wire; from another, over 2,000 oriental rugs.

(Leo J. Harris, 1999.)[5]

The Old Chicago Post Office and U.S. Custom House shown in a Lithograph from Chicago Souvenir Album.[6]

When they dismantled the old Chicago Post Office and Custom House in 1897, the building did not come down as easily as they hoped it would. They ended up dynamiting it, which shattered all the windows in the neighborhood.

The huge, 18-inch thick granite blocks that were salvaged from the Post Office were used to build the house I grew up in, and more importantly, the Basilica of St. Josephat in Milwaukee, Wisconsin, referred to as "Milwaukee's Catholic crown jewel." The basilica was designed by architect Erhard Brielmaier and modeled after St. Peter's Basilica in Rome.[7]

The Panama Canal Project

The Chicago House Wrecking Company salvaged and recycled, in 1911, a huge amount of material from the failed French attempt to build the Panama Canal, originally and unsuccessfully designed by De Lesseps. My father was in charge of that demolition project. He lived in Panama practically the entire year before I was born, directing the demolition. The locomotives and equipment had been left to rot in the jungle, and the

Dismantling the Chicago Post Office, February 9, 1897. My father, Frank Harris, is second from the right. His brother, Abraham Harris, the president of the company, is on the far right.

The Basilica of St. Josephat in Milwaukee was built with the stone from the old Post Office in Chicago.[8]

Chicago House Wrecking Company shipped them up, and sold them for their brass and copper content. This was a huge project for the company, and a very remunerative one. My nephew John shared the following information from his research in an email to the authors:

> The interest of the four Harris brothers in the canal building activities in Panama began in April of 1900. A letter dated March 21, 1906 from Panama City, from Samuel Harris to Frank Harris, went on in great detail about the availability of scrap metal and other salvage items that the then-bankrupt French contractors had abandoned.
>
> On September 5, 1911 bids were opened in Washington, D.C. for the purchase of all the French scrap remaining on the isthmus. The successful bidder was the Chicago House Wrecking Company (CHWC), which offered the sum of $215,000. The CHWC began work and employed 50 laborers under the supervision of four expatriate Americans, [including Frank Harris.] The work consisted of cleaning up the Mount Hope yards at Cristobal, and in clearing the way to outlying collections of scrap along the line of the Panama Railroad. The scrap collected was sorted into piles, amounting to about 40,000 tons, according to the grade of the metal. This material eventually was to be shipped directly to the foundries in the United States, who would purchase it from the CHWC. [9]
>
> During late August and early September 1912, the two sons of Frank Harris, Harvey Harris and Francis Harris, visited Cristobal. Harvey Harris described the piles of scrap at the Mount Hope Yards as "mountains of scrap thirty to forty feet high." [10]
>
> Controversy soon arose over interpreting the contract entered into by the CHWC. The CHWC sought all materials which originally belonged to the French contractors, but had been abandoned as junk. The CHWC insisted that this junk included many French barges, dredges, tugs, scows, launches, dump cars and railroad engines. In December of 1914 the matter was eventually resolved. The CHWC received 4,000 twelve-yard railroad dump cars and 700,000 pounds of scrap copper and brass, and as a part of the settlement relinquished all claims to the remainder of the materials. [11]
>
> (Leo J. Harris, 2014.)

In 1913, there was a reorganization of the Chicago House Wrecking Company in which they went public. This increased the capitalization and borrowing power of the resulting companies, including one called Harris Brothers Company that was to become the principal one in time. The focus of this business became catalogue mail-order sales of an astonishing variety of items—everything from lumber, hardware, clothing, office supplies, groceries, building materials, furniture, bathtubs, wire and fencing, machinery, plumbing fixtures, structural iron, and roofing materials to model house plans and kits. The company was a direct com-

My father, Frank Harris (right) at Mt. Hope, Cristobal, Panama, 1912.

The office of the Chicago House Wrecking Company, circa 1910. Sitting on desk, center right, with cap on, is my uncle, Dave Harris, the youngest of the four Harris Bothers.

The cover from a Chicago House Wrecking Company flyer.

petitor of Sears Roebuck & Company and Montgomery Ward.

The mail-order catalogs of these two companies are now collector's items, due to their striking design and impressive content. John notes that "[l]eading trade periodicals at the time have called these Chicago House Wrecking Company catalogs "remarkable" or "wonderfully interesting" since "a glance at the catalogue indicates that the company is in a position to supply on demand practically anything and everything."[12]

The sheer number of items offered for sale is staggering. Two of my relatives have been collecting the catalogs, buying them as they turn up on eBay from time to time. Not only do the catalogs include lengthy and detailed descriptions of each item, but there are page-long statements of the companies' business philosophy, practices, and guarantees—which are sometimes very humorous. For example, on page 7 of the Chicago House Wrecking Company 1909-1910 catalog #160 A, there appears the following paragraph:

Mistakes

If in your dealings with us you are confronted with a mistake we ask you to be patient. Remember your own faults. We have yet to meet "that perfect man." It's only human to make mistakes. If you want to show your manly nature then follow out the conduct that you would like were you the man who made the mistake and we the ones who had suffered. Write us the calm, cold facts in the case. Give us your order number, the date of your shipment, if you paid for the merchandise, and the date of your remittance and do everything you can to make the transaction plain to us. Then tell us just what your grievance is in plain, every-day English language. Do not resort to any abusive language in telling us the facts; reserve that until later on. We promise you that if you have had any injustice done you it will be properly righted. That's the way we expect to hold your trade and that's the way we expect to increase our business. If after you have written us all the facts in the case and we still refuse to give you justice you will have sufficient time to launch on us an avalanche of abuse.[13]

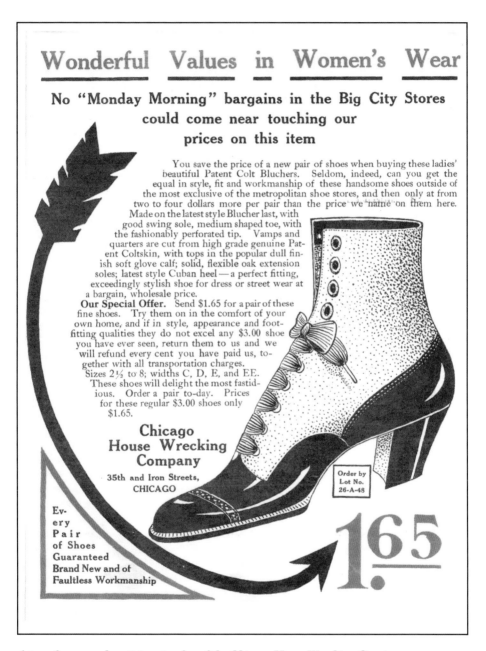

A page from an advertising circular of the Chicago House Wrecking Company.

A page from an advertising circular of the Chicago House Wrecking Company.

The 109-page Plan Book of Harris Homes pictured above from 1914 shows 86 different models of "cut-to fit" houses (and a few garages and barns) that can be bought in a kit, including the blueprints and all needed building materials, ranging in price from $398 to $1,179.

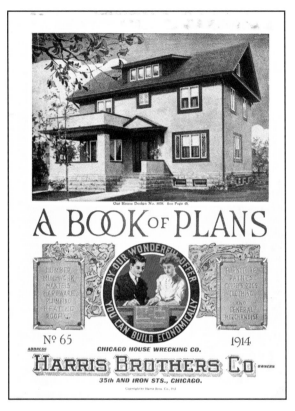

The cover of a Plan Book of Harris Homes from 1914.

It is not known how many house kits the Chicago House Wrecking Company and Harris Brothers Company sold, but their rival company, Sears, Roebuck & Co. sold about 70,000–75,000 homes through their mail order Modern Homes program between 1908 and 1940, which included 447 different housing variations.[14]

Harris Brothers Company was refinanced again around 1926 or 1927, and eventually the focus of the company shifted away from mail-order catalogs and pre-cut houses, and into lumber and millwork. The company was renamed Harris Crestline Company, and it manufactured doors and windows. The plant was located in Wisconsin.[15] The Harris family sold the Harris Crestline Company and its subsidiaries to the Sentry Insurance Company in 1981. Crestline windows and doors are still manufactured in Wisconsin and sold throughout the Midwest.[16]

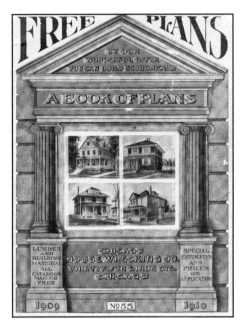

Covers from Chicago House Wrecking Company and Harris Brothers Company Catalogs.

FOOTNOTES

Introduction

1. Marilee Shapiro Asher, *My Story* (St. Paul: Pogo Press, 2011).

2. Marilee Shapiro Asher, *The Rest of My Story* (St. Paul: Pogo Press, 2013).

Chapter 3

1. "To Condemn Mansion," Hyde Park Herald, March 22, 1961, 1. Accessed September 20, 2014.

    http://nl.newsbank.com/nl-search/we/Archives/?p_product=HA-ILHPH&p_theme=histpaper&
    p_nbid=&p_action=doc&p_docid=13FFEB5CB43E3911&s_lastnonissuequeryname=5&d_viewref=
    search&p_queryname=5&p_docnum=7&toc=true&p_docref=v2:13EDAA8FD407386D@HA-ILHPH-
    13FFEB5C8C15D577@2437381-13FFEB5C92503597-13FFEB5CB43E3911

Chapter 5

1. For more information about Eleanor Harris' life and artwork, see Robert E. Asher and Leo J. Harris, *A Family of Artists* (St. Paul: Pogo Press, 1999).

2. Harvey L. Harris, *The War As I Saw It: 1918 Letters of a Tank Corps Lieutenant* (St. Paul: Pogo Press, 1998).

3. The following two articles reference Harvey Harris' involvement in cloud seeding:

    "Groups at Sterling and Hereford Back Cloud Seeding in Northeast" *Greeley Daily Tribune*, December 18, 1950, 7.

    http://www.newspapers.com/newspage/25061428/

    A Group of ranchers who met at Hereford Friday night express themselves as unanimously in favor of cloud seeding in north eastern Colorado. About $700 toward the project was raised at the meeting and other subscriptions were promised. The meeting was held at the Hereford Community hall under the auspices of the Crow Valley Farm Bureau. Glen Hodgell introduced the speaker, Jim Wilson of the A and M faculty at Fort Collins. A number of Hereford people attended the mass meeting at Sterling Thursday where $7500 was raised for the project. Colonel T. R. Gulenwaters addressed the Sterling meeting attended by about 800. He reported on the preliminary survey of the area. Harvey Harris, Sterling rancher, presided. It was estimated that rainfall in the northeast could be increased by five to seven inches above the annual average by cloud

*seeding. The survey indicated, Col. Gulenwaters said, that cloud seeding opera-
tions in the region could best be done from April thru September and October.
'The process, he added, should be closely coordinated with agricultural practices
in the region. As a general rule, Col. Gulenwaters said, his company would
refuse to seed clouds in the region during the late fall or winter season, but
under certain circumstances and with prospect of warm weather, there might be
periods in which winter operations would be justified and profitable.*

"Says Recent Snow Storm Was Seeded"
Greeley Daily Tribune, February 18, 1952, 9.

http://www.newspapers.com/newspage/27264287/ and
http://newspaperarchive.com/us/colorado/greeley/greeley-daily-tribune/1952/02-18/page-9

*Feb. 17—The possible explanation of the heavy snowfall this week in the Ster-
ling area of northeastern Colorado was suggested by Harvey L. Harris,
president of the Northeastern Colorado Water Development association, cloud
seeding by the Water Resources Development corporation of Denver. Although
sufficient funds have not been raised by the regional group to sign a new contract with the "rain-makers" Harris said the corporation agreed to seed any
likely-looking storm until February 15 as a goodwill gesture. Usual storm con-
ditions at this time of year are conducive to billiards, and no seeding would be
done; but Harris explained, because the "rain-makers" knew there would be
no winds they seeded the storm clouds. The three generators that were operated for this area were started at Klmnall, Neb., at midnight, Wednesday; at
Yuma at 1 p. m., Wednesday, and continued until 10:30 a. m., Thursday; and
at Brlggsdale in Weld county, at midnight, Thursday, and still operating Thursday evening, Harris said.*

[Author's note: Some typographical errors in the original documents were not changed.]

Chapter 6

1. PBS. American Experience. *"People & Events: The Leopold and
   Loeb Trial."* Accessed October 20, 2104.
   http://www.pbs.org/wgbh/amex/monkeytrial/peopleevents/e_leopoldloeb.html

2. Robert E. Asher and Charles Stuart Kennedy, *Interview with Robert E.
   Asher*, Association for Diplomatic Studies and Training, Foreign Affairs
   Oral History Project, Initial interview date: November 10, 2000.
   (Arlington, VA: ASTD, 2001). Used by permission.
   Accessed September 22, 2014.
   http://www.adst.org/OH%20TOCs/Asher,%20Robert%20E.toc.pdf

Chapter 7

1. Ford Burkhart, "Dr. Rachmiel Levine, 87, Diabetes Expert, Dies," *New York Times*, March 1, 1998.
   http://www.nytimes.com/1998/03/01/us/dr-rachmiel-levine-87-diabetes-expert-dies.html

2. Linda Crampton "Mary Poppins and a Biography of Her Creator, P. L. Travers," *HubPages*. August 29, 2014.
   http://hubpages.com/hub/Mary-Poppins-and-a-Biography-of-Her-Creator-P-L-Travers

3. Louise Anemaat, *"Guide to the papers of P. L. Travers in the Mitchell Library,"* State Library of New South Wales, Sydney, Australia, 1991.
   http://www.sl.nsw.gov.au/mssguide/ptravers.pdf

4. Robert E. Asher and Charles Stuart Kennedy, *Interview with Robert E. Asher*, Association for Diplomatic Studies and Training, Foreign Affairs Oral History Project. Initial interview date: November 10, 2000. (Arlington, VA: ASTD, 2001). Used by permission. Accessed September 22, 2014.
   http://www.adst.org/OH%20TOCs/Asher,%20Robert%20E.toc.pdf

Chapter 8

1. Wikipedia. "Works Progress Administration." Accessed Nov. 15, 2014.
   http://en.wikipedia.org/wiki/Works_Progress_Administration

2. Ibid.

3. Encyclopedia Britannica. "Alexander Archipenko." Accessed October 12, 2014.
   http://www.britannica.com/EBchecked/topic/32845/Alexander-Archipenko

4. Ibid.

5. Guggenheim Museum Collections Online. "Alexander Archipenko." Accessed October 12, 2014.
   http://www.guggenheim.org/new-york/collections/collection-online/artists/bios/553

6. Ingrid Rose and Roderick Quiroz, *The Lithographs of Prentiss Taylor: A Catalogue Raisonné.* (New York: Fordham University Press, 1996), 55. Accessed October 2014.
   https://books.google.com/books?id=Tp5qjyjVNd8C&pg=PA55&lpg=PA55&dq=Prentiss+Taylor+Washington+ARtists+Guild&source=bl&ots=BFPBqbjP0u&sig=631mfGEO5HFZlpVYrKwVZ4Molgg&hl=en&sa=X&ei=Iti_VOCuMsSiNrT7gJgG&ved=0CEUQ6AEwBg#v=onepage&q=Prentiss%20Taylor%20Washington%20ARtists%20Guild&f=false

7. Wikipedia. "Prentiss Taylor." Accessed October 12, 2014.

http://en.wikipedia.org/wiki/Prentiss_Taylor

8. Ibid.

9. Jane Watson, "Throng of Friendly Visitors Sees Washington Artists' Guild Exhibit," *Washington Post*, January 9, 1944, page 10-S. Accessed on Kenneth Stubbs Art.com. "*Washington Post* Review of 1944 Artists' Guild Group Exhibition." Accessed October 12, 2014.

http://kennethstubbsart.com/reviews/washingtonpost1944.html

10. The Cultural Tourism DC website on the Barnett Aden Gallery includes this description:

"The Barnett Aden Gallery, the first privately owned black gallery in the United States and one of Washington, DC's principal art galleries, was founded in 1943 by James Vernon Herring (1897-1969) and Alonzo Aden (1906-1961). Herring was chair of Howard University's Department of Art and Aden was curator of the Howard University Gallery of Art. The gallery was set up on the first floor of Herring's house, where he lived with Aden. The name Barnett honored Aden's mother's family. The Barnett Aden Gallery was central to the development and support of local and national artists and featured, among others, Elizabeth Catlett, Lois Mailou Jones, Alma Thomas, and Charles White. Aden and Herring were influenced by Alain Locke, whose 1925 The New Negro explored intellectual and philosophical approaches to art. While Aden, Herring, and Locke were all African Americans, the gallery was not conceived as a "black gallery." It was one of the few art spaces in the city in which artists representing different nationalities, races, and ethnicities were exhibited together. Noted for its afternoon art openings, the Barnett Aden Gallery became an important social gathering place."
Accessed October 14, 2014.

http://www.culturaltourismdc.org/portal/barnett-aden-gallery-african-american-heritage-trail#.VBh0SlYhxZg

Chapter 9

1. Wikipedia. "George Gurdjieff." Accessed December 1, 2014.

http://en.wikipedia.org/wiki/George_Gurdjieff

2. Gurdjieff Foundation Philadelphia. "About G. I. Gurdjieff." Accessed December 1, 2014.

http://gurdjieff-philadelphia.org/edit/about-g-i-gurdjieff/

3. Wikipedia. "George Gurdjieff." Accessed December 1, 2014.

http://en.wikipedia.org/wiki/George_Gurdjieff

Addendum

1. Leo J. Harris, "Wrecking to Save World's Fairs," *The Ephemera Journal*, 14:1, (Fall 2011); 1.

2. Samuel H. Harris, 'Wrecking to Save, not Destroy," *American Business Man*, June 1908, 267; quoted in Leo J. Harris, "Wrecking to Save—The Chicago House Wrecking Company," *Journal of the West*, 38:4 (October 1999); 65.

3. Leo J. Harris, "Wrecking to Save World's Fairs," *The Ephemera Journal*, 14:1, (Fall 2011); 4.

4. Ibid; 5-6.

5. Leo J. Harris, "Wrecking to Save—The Chicago House Wrecking Company," *Journal of the West*, 38:4 (October 1999); 66.

6. Old Chicago Post Office and U.S. Custom House. Accessed Oct. 1, 2014.
   http://patsabin.com/illinois/postoffice.htm

7. The Basilica of St. Josephat. "History of the Basilica." Accessed October 1, 2014.
   http://thebasilica.org/history

8. Ibid.

9. "Scrap Contractors at Work," *The Canal Record*, April 17, 1912.

10. Harvey Harris, in a letter to his mother Bonnie Harris, August 26, 1912.

11. Leo J. Harris, email message to authors, March 29, 2014.

12. "The Chicago House Wrecking Company," *The Iron Age* (Dec. 8, 1898), 45; "Farmers Buying at Wholesale," *The National Stockman and Farmer* 17 (Dec. 1, 1898), 17; and "A Unique Enterprise on a Huge Scale," *The Northwestern Lumberman* (Oct. 15, 1898), 11. Quoted in Leo J. Harris, "Wrecking to Save—The Chicago House Wrecking Company," *Journal of the West*, 38:4 (October 1999); 67.

13. Chicago House Wrecking Company 1909-1910 catalog #160A, page 7.

14. Sears Archives. "What is a Sears Modern Home?" Accessed February 26, 2015.
    http://www.searsarchives.com/homes/

15. Sears Modern Homes. "From House-wrecker to Home Maker: The Harris Brothers." Accessed October 9, 2014.
    http://www.searshomes.org/index.php/2011/02/10/from-house-wrecker-to-home-maker-the-harris-brothers/

16. Crestline Windows and Doors. Accessed October 9, 2014.
    http://www.crestlinewindows.com/wood.html

ENDNOTES

*Interested readers may wish to consult
the following family-related works:*

Harvey L. Harris, *The War as I Saw It: 1918 Letters of a Tank Corps Lieutenant.* (St. Paul: Pogo Press, 1998).

Leo J. Harris, "'Wrecking to Save—The Chicago House Wrecking Company." *Journal of the West,* 38:4 (October 1999) 65-74.

Leo J. Harris, "Wrecking to Save World's Fairs," *The Ephemera Journal* 14:1 (Fall 2011), 1-9.

Marilee Harris Shapiro Asher, *My Story* (St. Paul: Pogo Press, 2011).

Marilee Harris Shapiro Asher, *The Rest of My Story* (St. Paul: Pogo Press, 2013).

Robert E. Asher and Leo J. Harris. *A Family of Artists* (St. Paul: Pogo Press, 1999).

Robert E. Asher and Charles Stuart Kennedy, *Interview with Robert E. Asher,* Association for Diplomatic Studies and Training, Foreign Affairs Oral History Project. Interviewed by: Charles Stuart Kennedy Initial interview date: November 10, 2000. (Arlington, VA: ASTD, 2001).
http://www.adst.org/OH%20TOCs/Asher,%20Robert%20E.toc.pdf

*More of Marilee Shapiro Asher's artwork can be seen on her website,
www.marileeshapiro.com*

BOOK DESIGN AND LAYOUT BY KARLYN ROSEN AIRES, ELKINS PARK, PENNSYLVANIA

MARILEE SHAPIRO ASHER is an artist who resides in Washington, DC. Still vibrant and in good health physically and mentally at age 102, Marilee continues to create new work in sculpture, digital imaging and photography in her studio.

Back cover:
Marilee Shapiro Asher
The Way 2012
Bronze
14.5" x 11.5" x 2"

Made in the USA
Lexington, KY
01 December 2015